In Pursuit of Price Stability

The Wage-Price Freeze of 1971

STUDIES IN WAGE-PRICE POLICY

In Pursuit of Price Stability
The Wage-Price Freeze of 1971

ARNOLD R. WEBER

THE BROOKINGS INSTITUTION
Washington, D.C.

Library of Congress Cataloging in Publication Data:

Weber, Arnold Robert.
  In pursuit of price stability; the wage-price freeze of 1971.
  (Studies in wage-price policy)
  Includes bibliographical references.
  1. Wage-price policy—United States. I. Title.
II. Series.
HC110.W24W4   338.5′26′0973   73-11346

ISBN 0-8157-9264-6
ISBN 0-8157-9263-8 (pbk.)

9 8 7 6 5 4 3 2 1

THE BROOKINGS INSTITUTION is an independent organization devoted to nonpartisan research, education, and publication in economics, government, foreign policy, and the social sciences generally. Its principal purposes are to aid in the development of sound public policies and to promote public understanding of issues of national importance.

The Institution was founded on December 8, 1927, to merge the activities of the Institute for Government Research, founded in 1916, the Institute of Economics, founded in 1922, and the Robert Brookings Graduate School of Economics and Government, founded in 1924.

The Board of Trustees is responsible for the general administration of the Institution, while the immediate direction of the policies, program, and staff is vested in the President, assisted by an advisory committee of the officers and staff. The by-laws of the Institution state, "It is the function of the Trustees to make possible the conduct of scientific research, and publication, under the most favorable conditions, and to safeguard the independence of the research staff in the pursuit of their studies and in the publication of the results of such studies. It is not a part of their function to determine, control, or influence the conduct of particular investigations or the conclusions reached."

The President bears final responsibility for the decision to publish a manuscript as a Brookings book or staff paper. In reaching his judgment on the competence, accuracy, and objectivity of each study, the President is advised by the director of the appropriate research program and weighs the views of a panel of expert outside readers who report to him in confidence on the quality of the work. Publication of a work signifies that it is deemed to be a competent treatment worthy of public consideration; such publication does not imply endorsement of conclusions or recommendations contained in the study.

The Institution maintains its position of neutrality on issues of public policy in order to safeguard the intellectual freedom of the staff. Hence interpretations or conclusions in Brookings publications should be understood to be solely those of the author or authors and should not be attributed to the Institution, to its trustees, officers, or other staff members, or to the organizations that support its research.

Foreword

For generations, prosperity with price stability has been a cherished goal of Western industrialized nations. The pursuit of that goal confronts policy makers with technical requirements that are formidable enough. The quest is further complicated by political and institutional influences and constraints, notably the autonomous market power of large unions and corporations, the need for balancing political pressures against economic forces, and the obligation to act in awareness of that complex array of attitudes and apprehensions termed "expectations."

Many nations have experimented with various forms of "wage-price policies," or efforts by the government to influence directly the rate of increase of prices, wages, and other income shares. Such policies have been widely used by Western European countries since the Second World War. In the United States, the experience with these policies in peacetime has been more limited. From 1962 to 1966, the Kennedy and Johnson administrations made extensive use of wage and price guideposts explicitly stated by the Council of Economic Advisers. Although the guideposts were not legally enforceable, compliance with them was encouraged by intensive efforts at public education and by exhortation and persuasion.

On August 15, 1971, the Nixon administration took the unprecedented step of imposing direct, enforceable controls on wages, prices, and rents under economic conditions not significantly distorted by war. Phase I—a ninety-day freeze on wages and prices—constituted the first step in a series of controls that moved through Phases II and III and into Phase IV. The wage-price freeze of 1971 was comprehensive, and it enjoyed widespread public support. For some commentators it represented a proper, if belated, exercise of power by the government to check inflation. For others, it was a dangerous intervention that threatened free institutions and market efficiency. The record of those ninety days adds to the evidence needed to evaluate these contentions.

The Brookings Institution has had a continuing interest in the nature, management, and consequences of wage-price policy. In 1967, Brookings published John Sheahan's book *The Wage-Price Guideposts,* which analyzed the economic implications and administration of these policies during the Kennedy-Johnson period. The present study extends the review of experience in the United States by examining the origins and operations of the wage-price freeze of 1971. The author's primary responsibility for the management of the freeze and his strong scholarly interest in wage-price policies have enabled him to offer unique insights into the process of policy formulation and implementation.

This volume is the first of a series of studies that deal with the evolution of wage-price policies in the United States. The series is intended to contribute to public understanding of the purposes, problems, and consequences of governmental intervention into price- and wage-setting.

The manuscript profited greatly from the comments of Joseph A. Pechman, director of the Economic Studies Program at Brookings, and from those of John Sheahan, Phillip Cagan, and a third reader who remains anonymous. Further comments on factual content were provided by former staff members of the Cost of Living Council. Robert Erwin edited the manuscript; Evelyn P. Fisher checked the accuracy and consistency of data; and the index was prepared by Patricia P. B. Wells.

The views expressed in this volume are those of the author and should not be ascribed to the trustees, officers, or staff members of the Brookings Institution.

KERMIT GORDON
President

August 1973
Washington, D.C.

Author's Preface

The announcement of a wage-price freeze by President Nixon on August 15, 1971, was something new in American history. It set in motion a broad experiment in peacetime controls in the United States and removed the debate over "incomes policies" from the seminar room to the public domain. Direct controls over wages and prices now have joined monetary and fiscal policies as officially acknowledged remedies for dealing with the problems of inflation, employment, and growth. In the future, economic policy makers in the United States will be able to consider controls as one of the precedents in responding to political and economic pressures to maintain growth with price stability.

This volume provides a record of the wage-price freeze of 1971 and the steps that were taken to make it work. The study can be viewed at two levels. First, it incorporates an analysis of the specific policies that were formulated to give effect to the broad decision to put a lid on wages, prices, and rents. Second, it affords a detailed account of the administrative strategy and measures that were taken to translate the policies into an operative program. Though the greatest drama was associated with the imposition of the freeze itself, the credibility of the program was determined, in a large measure, by the performance of the leading players and the skill of the stagehands. This study does not attempt to deal in fine detail with the relationships between the freeze and complex economic variables and behavior. Those issues are best considered in an analytical framework encompassing the stabilization program in its entirety. Rather, emphasis is given to the process of policy formulation and implementation as it unfolded under conditions of extreme urgency.

Because I was Executive Director of the Cost of Living Council, the government unit that played the major role in the administration of the freeze, this study inevitably reflects ego as much as economics. However, I have strenuously attempted to avoid making this account either a memoir or a *mea culpa*. Indeed, the reader will probably conclude that when I was confronted with a choice between an insider's anecdote and dry analysis I opted for the academic virtues.

ix

The list of people who made an important contribution to the freeze—and hence this volume—is lengthier than can be accommodated here. But special mention should be made of a few. John B. Connally, Secretary of the Treasury and Chairman of the Cost of Living Council during the freeze, acted as anyone wants a boss to act; he made the big decisions quickly and unambiguously, backed up his staff when this was necessary, and gave it the latitude to do the job. George P. Shultz, then Director of the Office of Management and Budget, provided his customary good sense and support. George A. Lincoln, Director of the Office of Emergency Preparedness, carried out his responsibilities with the dedication and skill that distinguished a lifetime of service. Paul W. McCracken, Chairman of the Council of Economic Advisers, and Charls E. Walker, Under Secretary of the Treasury, lent their good judgment to the process of policy formulation every morning at eight o'clock. L. Patrick Gray III, Assistant Attorney-General, gave the full support of the Justice Department.

The greatest acknowledgment is extended to the hastily assembled members of the Cost of Living Council staff. In particular, Edgar R. Fiedler, Marvin H. Kosters, William Greener, Louis P. Neeb, William E. Nelson, and Malcolm Peterson deserve a large share of the credit for any success that the freeze enjoyed. Mrs. Gaye Lee also played a vital role in keeping the staff on an even keel with her grace and efficiency. Perhaps the largest debt is owed to Earl D. Rhode, whose brilliance and selflessness during the stabilization program was his last gift to the nation before his tragic death.

Last, while awaiting my return to Chicago, my wife Edna and sons David, Paul, and Robert demonstrated that there is no limit to familial patience and understanding.

A. R. W.

April 1973
Chicago, Illinois

Contents

In Pursuit of Price Stability
The Wage-Price Freeze of 1971

Abbreviations

ASCS Agricultural Stabilization and Conservation Service
BLS Bureau of Labor Statistics
CEA Council of Economic Advisers
CISC Construction Industry Stabilization Committee
CLC Cost of Living Council
EPC Executive Policy Committee of the Cost of Living Council
FMC Federal Maritime Commission
FRB Board of Governors of the Federal Reserve System
IATA International Air Transport Association
IRS Internal Revenue Service
OEP Office of Emergency Preparedness
OMB Office of Management and Budget
TECA Temporary Emergency Court of Appeals
USDA U.S. Department of Agriculture
USDL U.S. Department of Labor

I

The Background

On August 15, 1971, President Nixon announced the imposition of a comprehensive freeze on wages, prices, and rents. The freeze descended like an avalanche rather than a glacier and was initiated without warning or public discussion. It marked the first time that direct wage and price controls had been instituted in the United States under peacetime conditions and was the initial step in an extensive experiment with incomes policies.

Though the wage-price freeze appeared to be precipitate, it reflected economic and political developments that often have been the prelude to the introduction of incomes policies in other countries. From the outset of the Nixon administration the suppression of inflation had been a central concern. In 1969, the first year of the new administration, consumer prices rose at an annual rate of 6.1 percent. Inflation subsided only slightly during 1970, when the consumer price index increased by 5.5 percent. In attempting to moderate these price movements, the administration adopted a policy of "gradualism" whereby it was hoped prices would be brought under control without incurring a significant increase in unemployment or unduly dampening economic growth. If the surge of price increases that took place through 1969 and 1970 posed a political threat to the administration, the existence of full employment constituted a resource to be conserved to the maximum.

This strategy showed poor results; a solution to the problem of achieving full employment with relative price stability proved to be highly elusive. By the end of 1970, unemployment had risen to 6 percent, and the rate fluctuated in a narrow range through the first seven months of 1971. To be sure, a significant portion of this jump in unemployment could be attributed to the reduction in the size of the armed forces and the cutback in defense production.[1] Nonetheless, this observation did not alleviate the social or political consequences of the deterioration of labor market conditions.

In the first seven months of 1971 there was some hope that the rate of

1. According to a study by the U.S. Bureau of Labor Statistics, the cutbacks in the armed forces and military production, beginning in 1969, resulted in the loss of 1.5 million jobs. See Richard P. Oliver, "Employment Effects of Reduced Defense Spending," *Monthly Labor Review,* Vol. 94 (December 1971), pp. 3–11.

inflation was receding. From December 1970 to August 1971 the consumer price index rose at an annual rate of 3.8 percent, the best performance for that period of the year since 1967. However, other evidence stirred concern that the administration's efforts to control inflation were inconclusive. Despite the decline in the rate of increase in the consumer price index, the wholesale price index had risen at a 5.2 percent annual rate in the first seven months of 1971, as compared to 2.2 percent for all of 1970. Furthermore, the price deflator for gross private product had increased from 4.5 in 1970 to an annual rate of 5.0 percent in the early part of 1971. These developments presented a mixed picture and did not blunt the criticisms of the existing "game plan."

If the increase in unemployment provided a somber background for the slow reduction in the rate of price increase, this softening in the labor market could be expected to provide a bright spot by slowing upward wage movements. Throughout 1969 and 1970, collective bargaining settlements had risen to high levels. By the end of 1970 the average first-year increase in newly negotiated collective bargaining contracts was in excess of 8 percent. But the bright spot did not appear. Collective bargaining developments in 1971 indicated that little relief was in prospect. The settlement in the can industry in the spring of 1971 set a generous mark that became a target in aluminum and steel, resulting in first-year settlements calling for an estimated 16 percent hike in compensation costs. The prolonged work rules dispute in the railroad industry ground to an expensive, if not constructive, conclusion which permitted wages to increase more than 40 percent over the 42 months beginning January 1, 1970. In the second quarter of 1971, the average first-year increase for major collective bargaining settlements was 10 percent.[2]

In part, expectations that unemployment would moderate the unions' demands proved to be wrong because the relationship between the bargaining cycle and the business cycle had altered the climate for wage negotiations. Most of the large bargaining units now operated under three-year agreements. This meant that many of the unions whose contracts expired during 1971 were intent on achieving at least "catch up" increases to compensate for the recent inflation. On the other hand, if a particular

2. U.S. Bureau of Labor Statistics, *Current Wage Developments,* No. 282 (July 1971), p. 2, and No. 297 (October 1972), p. 38.

According to U.S. Department of Labor News Release 71-416, July 29, 1971, the average first-year increase for wages *and benefits* was 10.4 percent of the first six months of 1971.

union had managed to protect the economic position of its members because previous wage increases had been sufficiently generous, the expectation of continued price inflation generated strong pressures to obtain a cushion through the duration of the new contract. These considerations were especially consequential in those situations where a labor agreement did not include an escalator clause providing for the upward adjustment of wages in response to changes in the consumer price index during the contract term. In this manner, wage rates might keep rising by an amount larger than was justified by demand conditions, thereby prolonging inflation.

Thus in the summer of 1971 the measures of economic activity stood in painful proximity. Price trends were mixed, and vigorous pressures were still exerted on costs by sizable wage increases. Deflationary measures to deal with the situation were infeasible or politically perilous. The budget for the fiscal year 1971 showed a deficit in excess of $20 billion; at the same time the money supply was increasing at a prodigious rate, partly in response to nudging by the administration. Any strenuous efforts to change these developments ran the risk of increasing unemployment to unacceptable levels in terms of political and national economic requirements.

Political factors also worked to reduce the administration's discretion in the exercise of new policy options. Throughout his administration, the President and his chief economic advisers had steadfastly resisted demands for a more activist policy in the wage and price area. This clamor for action was met with statements from the administration that pressure tactics such as "jawboning" and related measures didn't work, that even if they should work they distorted the allocative processes of the economy and constituted an intrusion on the exercise of essential freedoms. In his *Economic Report* submitted to the Congress on February 1, 1971, the President had stated, "I do not intend to impose wage and price controls. . . . Neither do I intend to rely upon an elaborate facade that seems to be wage and price control but is not."[3]

At the same time that the administration was opposing economic activism, it was taking some steps "to show the flag" to minimize the demands for more bellicose action in the labor and product markets. In the spring of 1970, a National Commission on Productivity was established, composed of representatives from business, labor, the public, and government. In addition, it was announced that "inflation alerts" would be sounded by

3. *Economic Report of the President, February 1971*, p. 7.

the Council of Economic Advisers when particular price or wage actions endangered the battle for price stability.[4] Neither of these measures had any noticeable effect on events.

A few restrained efforts at jawboning were made as time went on. Modifying a general policy of aloofness from collective bargaining disputes, the President did personally intervene in labor negotiations in the railroad and steel industries. The form of the Presidential intervention was relatively mild, however, and was limited to summoning the parties to the White House and exhorting them to engage in responsible collective bargaining.

In both cases, this genteel exercise in jawboning did contribute to settlements without a strike but did little to relieve the pressure on the economy in view of the fact that the two agreements were concluded with generous wage settlements. Any disposition to be "tough" was mitigated by the experience in the late fall of 1970 when the extended strike in the automobile industry appeared to have dealt a setback to efforts to restore a high level of economic expansion.

One special case did provide evidence that the administration was willing to take decisive action to relieve what it viewed as intolerable wage developments. Beginning in late 1967, wages in the construction industry experienced a sharp upsurge subsequently characterized as an "explosion." To encircle the problem, a Cabinet Committee on Construction was established under the chairmanship of the Secretary of Labor in September 1969, and later that month the Construction Industry Collective Bargaining Commission, with representatives of management, labor, and government, was formed by executive order. Neither of these measures had the desired effect, and finally in February 1971 the President suspended the provisions of the Davis-Bacon Act which had long been used to protect and extend union wage scales in federal construction. The Davis-Bacon Act provided that "prevailing rates" should be paid for construction financed by the federal government. In most cases, the "prevailing rate" was defined as the union rate for particular crafts. The suspension of the act was viewed as a drastic measure and paved the way for the establish-

4. "Economic Policy and Productivity," text of the President's June 17, 1970, statement, *Weekly Compilation of Presidential Documents,* Vol. 6 (June 22, 1970), p. 777.

On the changed doctrine behind the freeze, see "The Challenge of Peace," text of the President's August 15, 1971, radio and television address, *Weekly Compilation of Presidential Documents,* Vol. 7 (August 23, 1971), pp. 1168–72.

ment of the Construction Industry Stabilization Committee (CISC) at the end of March 1971.

Ironically, the CISC was established under the authority of the Economic Stabilization Act whose extension the administration had reluctantly accepted one month before. The committee, tripartite in nature and empowered to regulate collective bargaining settlements, was dealing with an industry which, in 1970, had provided for median first-year wage increases of approximately 17 percent.[5] It is noteworthy that CISC was accepted with little controversy by the AFL-CIO and the national leaders of the construction unions, who tacitly recognized that wage movements in the industry had gotten out of control. In addition, considerable preparatory work had been carried out by Professor John T. Dunlop of Harvard University, who subsequently was named chairman of the CISC.

These actions did little to reduce the administration's political vulnerability to criticism. At first, the sniping came from organized labor and the Congress. Both heavily played the "worst of all worlds" theme, and in 1971 the AFL-CIO was calling for the imposition of wage and price controls.[6] As early as August 1970, Congress had enacted the Economic Stabilization Act as an amendment to the Defense Production Act. The stabilization act was passed over the strenuous opposition of the administration and probably was designed to embarrass rather than to be exercised. It gave the President sweeping power to stabilize wages, prices, and rents without recourse to the Congress and left him unfettered by any procedural niceties. The act was extended in May 1971, this time through April 30, 1972.

Statements from the business community, the Chairman of the Board of Governors of the Federal Reserve System, and the press amplified the sniping to a broad fusillade in the spring and early summer of 1971. The emergence of Arthur Burns as an advocate for incomes policies had a

5. By the fourth quarter of 1971, the median annual first-year wage percentage increase in major union contracts in the construction industry was 13. *Current Wage Developments,* No. 282 (July 1971), p. 57, and No. 297 (October 1972), p. 62.

6. Appearing on the television show "Meet the Press" in July 1971, George Meany, President of the AFL-CIO, stated, "I can tell you this: if I was in his [President Nixon's] position, I would impose controls at this time. I don't see any other way that this situation is going to get under control." Bureau of National Affairs, *Daily Labor Report,* No. 133 (July 12, 1971), p. A-6.

On August 10, 1971—five days before the freeze—the AFL-CIO Executive Council adopted the following statement: "We are prepared to cooperate with mandatory government controls, if the President decides they are necessary, provided such controls are evenhanded and across-the-board." *Daily Labor Report,* No. 154 (August 10, 1971), p. A-15.

particularly significant impact on the politics of economic policy. Burns had been a top White House adviser during the first year of the Nixon administration and had impeccable credentials as a conservative economist. When he became Chairman of the Board of Governors of the Federal Reserve, it was expected that he would continue to be a strong supporter of the administration's policies, even granted the independent status of the Federal Reserve Board. Beginning in December 1970, however, Burns became increasingly critical of the administration's strategy to deal with inflation. In a speech delivered at Pepperdine College, Burns listed a variety of measures that could be used to dampen inflation.[7] Among these suggested measures was a high-level Price and Wage Review Board that would have broad authority to investigate price and wage changes and to make recommendations for adjustments.

Burns expanded his advocacy of incomes policies in subsequent appearances before Congressional committees in February and April 1971. In exchanges with Senator William Proxmire, who was one of the indefatigable critics of the administration's policies, Burns asserted that the economy was confronted by a "new problem" and that he was "inclined to think" a price and wage review board would be helpful in curbing inflation.[8] Burns' public diagnosis that the "old game plan" was inadequate for solving the "new problem" had reverberations in the White House and lent respectability to the demands for instituting some form of incomes policy.

Further support for active government intervention to restrain wage and price increases was forthcoming from the business community. At a meeting of the Business Council in October 1970, the chief economic spokesmen for the administration were subjected to harsh criticisms for failing to check excessive wage increases and price inflation. The fact that the Business Council was comprised of the top executives of the largest corporations in the nation indicated that the administration could not dispel demands for economic activism by appeals to conservative ideology. This corporate expression of discontent was conveyed directly to the President by a committee of the council and was reaffirmed at the next council meeting in the spring of 1971. In a large measure, the business attitudes ap-

7. For a listing of the measures, see *The 1971 Economic Report of the President,* Hearings before the Joint Economic Committee, 92 Cong. 1 sess. (1971), Pt. 1, pp. 249–50.

8. "Statement of Hon. Arthur F. Burns, Chairman, Board of Governors, Federal Reserve System," in *ibid.,* pp. 244–45.

peared to reflect a frustration in coping with unions in collective bargaining, but they found more neutral expression in a demand for some form of comprehensive incomes policy.

Despite these criticisms and the fact that the administration had been edging toward more direct efforts to deal with wage and price developments, White House rhetoric continued to disparage incomes policies. It was a set of proximate causes in the international area that moved the President to impose a wage-price freeze. What was unpalatable when served up by itself became an important element in a more comprehensive menu for dealing with the economy's disabilities. With one great step, the administration could dissipate the political pressures at home while seizing the initiative in its dealings with its economic partners abroad.

The proximate developments were the steady deterioration of the balance of payments and the attack on the dollar in international money markets. The deficit in the U.S. balance of payments had been increasing steadily in the past year and registered a significant increase in the second and third quarters of 1971, as shown in Table 1. By the summer of 1971, the dollar came under heavy pressure from abroad. On the domestic scene, the basic steel producers and the United Steelworkers of America on August 1 reached a new labor agreement calling for an immediate increase of 15 percent in wage and fringe benefits, an indicator that cost-push pressures had not abated.

At the beginning of August the President and his top economic advisers started to put together a comprehensive plan of economic action that would deal with both the domestic and international incubi. The major elements in the plan were the levying of a surcharge on imports, the suspension of the convertibility of the dollar for gold, and various tax measures. These measures might be expected to have a salutary effect upon unemployment; however, they offered little relief with regard to the price situation. Indeed,

Table 1. *U.S. Balance of Payments, 1971*
Millions of dollars

Quarter of the year	Balance on goods and services	Balance on current account	Balance on current account and long-term capital
1st	1,136	345	−1,279
2d	36	−810	−2,999
3d	91	−855	−3,296
4th	−537	−1,529	−1,732

Source: U.S. Bureau of Economic Analysis, *Business Conditions Digest* (February 1973), p. 87.

through imposing the surcharge and permitting the value of the dollar to float downward, the discipline on domestic product markets would be loosened, creating a further likelihood of domestic price increases. Against this background, an important short-term element in the administration's change of economic policy was the imposition of a wage-price freeze. Some staff work on the form and feasibility of incomes policies had been initiated independently by the Council of Economic Advisers and the Federal Reserve Board. However, a specific request for a presentation of options was not forthcoming from the White House until the first week in August, and then the assignment was given to the Office of Management and Budget in the Executive Office of the President. The pretext for the earlier staff work was the preparation of testimony that OMB Director George Shultz was scheduled to give before the Joint Economic Committee of Congress in September.[9]

When the President called his top economic advisers to a meeting at Camp David on August 13, the broad decision to impose a wage-price freeze was reached on the first day. This determination reflected the conviction that if the administration lost its virtue with respect to incomes policies, it should enjoy the full benefits of its transgressions by acting decisively and with immediately perceptible effect. The general details of the freeze were developed by a working group composed of Burns of the Federal Reserve, Paul McCracken of the Council of Economic Advisers, and Arnold R. Weber, the Associate Director of the Office of Management and Budget. This group accepted in principle a blueprint for the freeze as proposed in the staff document prepared by OMB. The OMB analysis also recommended the establishment of a tripartite wage-price review board when the freeze terminated. This board would have been authorized to review and make recommendations concerning wage and price increases and, further, could impose selective controls if necessary. The working group rejected this approach as premature and agreed that the structure of the longer-term incomes policy should not be decided until the reaction of the public to the freeze could be gauged and various interest groups canvassed.

The recommendations of the working group were then brought to the President and were approved with some modifications concerning coverage and duration. The President concurred in the recommendation to exclude

9. The planning memorandum was prepared by William H. Kolberg, Assistant Director of OMB, and Earl D. Rhode, Special Assistant to the Associate Director of OMB. I supervised the preparation of the document.

"raw" agricultural products from the freeze but extended the duration of Phase I, as the initital period of controls was christened, from 60 to 90 days. He particularly supported the judgment that the nature of the post-freeze program should not be determined until there had been public discussion of the issues. On August 15, the administration vaulted across ideological and historical barriers and imposed a comprehensive 90-day freeze on wages, salaries, prices, and rents. It further imposed a 10 percent surcharge on imports and suspended the convertibility of dollars to gold.

Thus, despite the element of surprise, the imposition of the freeze was not a capricious act taken to confound critics or to confuse political antagonists. In many ways, it reflected the "traditional" set of variables that had led to such actions in other Western countries, i.e., persistent inflation, balance-of-payments difficulties, and an unwillingness or inability to adopt deflationary measures because of the impact of such measures on employment.

The unique aspect of these direct controls lies in the fact that they were initiated under peacetime conditions when the economy was operating at significantly less than full capacity in the product and labor markets. To some extent, however, this circumstance made incomes policy more viable by permitting the administration to exert pressure on institutional wage- and price-fixing arrangements at a time when downward pressure was less likely to be overwhelmed by fiscal and monetary forces. In addition, the administration had so reduced its options by engaging in symbolic forms of intervention which were generally ineffective that much stronger medicine had to be used. By resisting the imposition of some form of incomes policy so long and so stridently, the administration, paradoxically, had increased the inevitability of resorting to such policies and expanding their scope. Whereas a wage and price review board or some voluntary mechanism for restraint might have sufficed earlier, the situation in the summer of 1971 seemed to require bolder measures in both political and economic terms.

II

Incomes Policy and the
Wage-Price Freeze

The wage-price freeze of 1971 was a massive application of one variant of those economic remedies characterized as "incomes policies." These policies have been loosely defined in both theory and practice. The enthusiastic public response to the President's initiative in August 1971 probably reflected an appreciation of his resolve to vanquish inflation rather than an understanding of the technical dimensions of the economic stabilization program.

The term "incomes policy" generally has been employed to describe those governmental actions, other than fiscal and monetary measures, that are designed to control the rate of increase of wages, prices, and other forms of income. Some commentators have expanded the definition to include structural changes in the economy that are intended to diminish upward presssure on prices and wages.[1] As a matter of usage, however, incomes policies usually are limited to efforts to influence wage and price movements directly. There is no a priori taxonomy for incomes policies, but experience in the United States and abroad indicates that they run the gamut from mere exhortation to the outright statutory regulation of wage and price decisions by complex bureaucratic procedures.[2] Between these polar positions, the different types of incomes policy can be distinguished by reference to four criteria: coverage, the nature of the standard, methods for inducing compliance, and duration.

1. This was the position taken by Arthur Burns in his Pepperdine College speech. See *New York Times,* December 7, 1970.
2. For a comprehensive discussion of the varieties of incomes policies used in various Western European nations, see Lloyd Ulman and Robert J. Flanagan, *Wage Restraint: A Study of Incomes Policies in Western Europe* (University of California Press, 1971). A useful taxonomy of incomes policies as developed in the United States and abroad is found in David C. Smith, *Incomes Policies: Some Foreign Experiences and Their Relevance for Canada* (Ottawa: Queen's Printer and Controller of Stationery, 1966).

Dimensions of Policy

Coverage. The coverage of any form of incomes policy will most directly express the theory underlying the initiation of the policy. Thus a judgment that price inflation has been the consequence of cost-push factors generally implies that the remedial measures will focus not on the economy as a whole but on those "centers of power" that presumably can exercise an autonomous influence on wage and price movements. In contrast, a diagnosis of demand-pull inflation is likely to result in the comprehensive coverage of broad sectors of the economy by any program designed to curb wage and price increases. Extensive coverage is also likely to result from an expectational theory of inflation whereby wages and prices are believed to rise because of expectations that gains in money wages and profits will be eroded by increases in the cost of living and factor prices. Under these circumstances, the broad application of incomes policy may be considered necessary to break the chain of expectations. In any case, the coverage of an incomes policy is subject to almost infinite variation, from individual firms to the entire economy, depending upon the assumptions and objectives of the program.

The Nature of the Standard. Any form of incomes policy requires a standard of performance to control or influence the behavior of economic decision makers. In its vaguest form, the standard may call for "wage restraint" or "a responsible price policy." Here, the standard is little more than an admonition with highly ambiguous operational implications. The policy makers may adopt this approach purposefully to create uncertainty or the illusion of affirmative government actions without developing a specific program. It is hoped that this uncertainty or illusion of intervention will result in conservative behavior in labor and product markets without requiring more forthright measures.[3]

The standard for wage or price behavior may be more precise conceptually without providing firm arithmetic guidance. For example, the standard for acceptable wage increases may be defined in terms of the long-term rate of increase in labor productivity. While the concept of long-term labor productivity is generally understood, its translation into a specific

3. This approach appeared to be implicit in Phase III of the Economic Stabilization Program, initiated in January 1973. Although the government formally adhered to a 5.5 percent wage standard, considerable rhetoric was expended to emphasize its "flexibility."

number may still be subject to significant variance. Under the Kennedy and Johnson administrations, the wage guideline was linked to national average increases in productivity, but there was a major difference of opinion over whether the government should choose a figure on the basis of the entire postwar period or employ a five-year moving average.[4] The use of a conceptual standard related to some economic variable helps to refine the guidance given to private decision makers while permitting some variation over time or in particular cases. In some cases, this variation will reflect bargaining factors rather than ambiguity in the concept itself.

Still more concretely, the standard may be expressed in terms of an explicit number: for example, wage gains restricted to 3 percent and price increases to 1 percent. Such a number not only limits the behavior of economic units but also establishes a precise goal for the program as well. A specific numerical standard is most likely to be promulgated as part of a comprehensive stabilization program in order to satisfy demands for even-handed treatment while facilitating general compliance.

The nature of the standard will be further elaborated by the policy toward exceptions. If the standard is viewed as a target for the performance of the economy as a whole, some firms or groups of workers may be permitted to exceed the standard in the expectation that others will fall short of the allowable amount. Consequently, some criteria will have to be developed governing the incidence and magnitude of the exceptions. These criteria, in turn, will be related to the level of the standard in the light of recent wage and price movements. The policy toward exceptions is likely to be permissive when a tight standard is in effect; conversely, when there is a loose standard, a stringent policy toward exceptions probably will be adopted. This relationship reflects the obvious fact that a tight standard is infeasible or undesirable to maintain in a complex economy, whereas a loose standard affords greater latitude for making wage and price adjustments that are necessary to promote the efficient allocation of resources.

Methods for Gaining Compliance. The nature of incomes policy will also be determined by the methods used to bring about compliance with the standard. All the methods essentially involve the application of some form of sanctions. The possible sanctions are infinite in variety and are limited only by the ingenuity of government officials. In general, they fall into three categories: the mobilization of public opinion, threatened re-

---

4. For a discussion of this issue, see *Economic Report of the President, together with the Annual Report of the Council of Economic Advisers, January 1966,* pp. 91–93.

prisals such as the withdrawal of certain benefits, or legal restraints and penalties including court injunctions and fines.

The methods of compliance that are actually used are related to the decisions that have been made concerning coverage and the nature of the standard. The broader the coverage of the incomes policy, the more likely that formal legal sanctions will be sought. It is doubtful that jawboning can be exercised in other than a few, highly visible situations or that public opinion can be mobilized to bring the corner grocer to bay. This observation implies that informal sanctions are best used when the coverage of the incomes policy is limited. Similarly, general guidelines or exhortations for "responsibility" are not amenable to legal enforcement. Instead, experience in the United States and abroad indicates that where vague standards of economic behavior are invoked, they are supported by efforts to arouse public opinion against those who appear to violate the standard.

On the other hand, the adoption of an explicit, arithmetic standard will increase the need for a formal system of compliance supported by legal sanctions. In the absence of these sanctions, major breaches of the standard may occur and publicly signal the ineffectiveness of the stabilization program. This sequence of events took place in 1966 when the wage guidelines favored by the government were ignored in the wake of a settlement between the International Association of Machinists and United Airlines that called for a pay hike of about 5 percent—far in excess of the then current 3.2 percent standard.[5]

Beyond these technical considerations, the selection of the appropriate method for gaining compliance must be tailored to public support for the incomes policy. It is correct that the stronger the public support for the policy, the more formal and punitive the sanctions can be. Paradoxically, however, when there is widespread public support, the need for the exercise of stiff sanctions will probably be unnecessary. In contrast, it will be difficult to sustain legal methods for gaining compliance when the public's enthusiasm for the program is restrained. In these circumstances, the limited support must be nurtured and conserved and can best be used selectively through informal sanctions, such as jawboning.

Duration. The duration of any exercise in incomes policy is obviously related to the persistence of the economic conditions that the policy is designed to remedy. Nevertheless, some limitations will be posed by tech-

5. For a discussion of this incident, see John Sheahan, *The Wage-Price Guideposts* (Brookings Institution, 1967), pp. 57–60.

nical and tactical factors associated with the characteristics of the incomes policy that is adopted. As a practical matter, it will be difficult to sustain a stabilization program over a long period of time when the program is marked by comprehensive coverage, a tight standard, and punitive means of compliance. Under these conditions, economic distortions, widespread evasion, and public resentment are likely to develop such that the policy will have to be modified or discarded. It is true that during wartime appeals to patriotism and national survival will often provide the discipline necessary to support the rigorous application of controls. Even in this case, however, the continuance of controls is likely to give rise to black markets and related efforts at evasion. And once hostilities have been terminated, the pressures for junking the program usually are irresistible. Within the American experience, it is instructive to note that the World War II controls were overturned shortly after the end of the war despite some efforts to keep them in place. During the Korean War, when public support for controls was always precarious, continued adjustments had to be made to preserve the system of wage and price controls for the duration of the conflict.

The use of wage guidelines in the United States also sheds some light on the relationship between the duration and other aspects of incomes policies. The 1962–66 standard was linked to national average increases in productivity, with latitude for significant exceptions. Coverage was formally comprehensive, but, in fact, close attention was given only to highly visible pricing situations and collective bargaining settlements in large units. Compliance was generally achieved by exhortation and the manipulation of public opinion. Through this combination of flexibility, selectivity, and informal pressure the wage guidelines were maintained for four years before they were undermined by economic events.[6]

Whatever decisions are made concerning the duration of the incomes policy, it is probably desirable to maintain public uncertainty at the outset. When private decision makers are aware that a program will terminate at a specified time, this prospect will influence wage and price behavior in such a manner that the effect of the program is more likely to defer rather than to dampen any increases. One of the most troublesome aspects of incomes policy is the tendency for a wage and price "explosion" to occur when the program of controls is ended.

6. Sheahan, *ibid.,* provides the best narrative and analysis of experience with the guideposts.

The Nature of a Wage-Price Freeze

Of the four dimensions of incomes policy, the distinguishing character-istic of a wage-price freeze is the nature of the standard. As the metaphor implies, a "freeze" envisions a zero standard of permissible increases. Some wage and price movements may be allowed, but they are more likely to represent technical interpretations of the detailed regulations governing the freeze rather than any flexibility in the standard.

The rigorous nature of the standard does not theoretically dictate the scope of coverage. In principle, a freeze may be applied on a selective basis to particular industries or incomes shares. However, to the extent that in-comes policies are designed to deal with inflationary pressures in the econ-omy in general, there is a clear implication that a freeze will be compre-hensive when it is imposed. Technically, if some prices and wages are frozen while others are permitted to rise, it is difficult to avoid disruptive consequences for output because of rising raw material costs and the loss of labor. In addition, equitable considerations make it politically perilous to impose an absolute limit on one sector of the economy or income share and not others. If a freeze is limited to one income share, prices rather than wages are most likely to be the focus of the program of restraint. On the one hand, there usually will be broad political support for a ceiling on prices and not wages. On the other hand, it is presumed that freezing prices will stiffen management's resistance to wage demands or reduce labor's appetite for large wage increases.

When a freeze was imposed in the United Kingdom in 1966 and again in 1972, the controls encompassed both wages and prices. A similar ap-proach was taken in Denmark in 1963. In contrast, the scope of the freeze was limited to prices alone in Sweden in 1970 and Norway in 1972. Per-haps the most discriminating application of a freeze occurred in France in 1963. Here, the ban on price increases was restricted to manufactured goods while rollbacks were ordered for the prices of cigarettes, beefsteak, and gasoline.[7] As far as can be determined, no Western industrialized na-tions since World War II have frozen wages and not prices.

A freeze will be relatively short-lived and is seldom more than six months in duration. The maximum feasible period will vary with the cover-age of the freeze and the complexity of the economy to which it is applied.

7. Organisation for Economic Cooperation and Development, *Economic Surveys by the OECD: France* (Paris, 1964), pp. 27–28.

Although there is no set formula, a comprehensive freeze cannot be sustained for long in a modern economy without having severe effects on resource allocation or engendering severe political strains. In addition, a freeze may disadvantage labor by permitting management to reap the immediate gains from increases in productivity by barring wage increases that otherwise would reflect this factor. Thus the wage-price freezes imposed in the United Kingdom were limited to six months in 1966 and three months in 1972. In Sweden, the price freeze alone was maintained for ten months during 1970–71. The longest wage-price freeze was probably the one imposed in Denmark in 1963–65. The freeze was formally maintained for two years, although various exceptions were made to permit wage and price adjustments during this period.[8]

The methods for gaining compliance during a freeze can be highly variable. If the standard is relatively simple, voluntary compliance can be promoted by an active propaganda campaign. Unless the policy makers have seriously misjudged the extent of the national consensus supporting the freeze, appeals for voluntary compliance generally will be adequate to sustain the program. Legal enforcement powers may be sought and utilized to display "toughness" in individual cases or to bolster the freeze as it progresses. In most cases where a wage-price freeze has been imposed, primary reliance has been placed on appeals for voluntary cooperation rather than legal methods for gaining compliance.

The U.S. wage-price freeze of 1971 generally conformed to the theoretical and empirical characteristics of this variant of incomes policy. A standard of zero was established for permissible wage and price increases. Coverage was comprehensive, with only one significant exemption—raw agricultural products. The duration of the freeze was limited to 90 days. Legal sanctions were available to enforce the program, but primary emphasis was given to exhortation and intensive efforts to enlist public support.

The Uses of a Wage-Price Freeze

As the most drastic form of incomes policy, the objectives of a wage-price freeze tend to be limited and short-term in nature. A wage-price

8. Organisation for Economic Cooperation and Development, *Economic Surveys by the OECD: Denmark* (Paris, 1964), pp. 6–7. Under the terms of the Danish freeze, the wages of low-pay workers were permitted to increase by 1.25 percent the first year and 2.5 percent the second year.

freeze is more of a blunderbuss than a surgical instrument and cannot be utilized in a sophisticated manner to deal with either cost-push or demand-pull inflation. Whatever the operational shortcomings of incomes policies may be as a device to guide or modify behavior in a complex economy, they probably are accentuated where a freeze is involved.

As an economic policy designed to influence wage and price movements, a freeze is most significant as an effort to modify expectations. By signifying the government's resolve to bring inflation under control, wage and price increases that reflect the expectation that real wage gains will decline and costs will rise may be dampened, albeit temporarily. The long-run task of achieving economic growth with wage and price stability obviously requires the application of monetary and fiscal policies and—many commentators would maintain—incomes policies that are more sophisticated than a wage-price freeze. For the public at large or major economic interest groups, however, these policies are arcane, and their salutary impact, if any, is revealed only after a time lag of some duration. Consequently, a freeze can be a useful instrument to achieve an immediate change in expectations. In Sweden, one of the primary objectives of the price freeze of 1970 was to influence forthcoming labor negotiations. Because a national wage agreement is negotiated between the trade union and employer federations in Sweden, it was important to minimize the unions' expectations of price increases in order to limit their wage demands.[9] Similar considerations were applicable in Denmark in 1963.

Although a fragile economic theory may be articulated to explain or justify the imposition of a wage-price freeze, the objective is more likely to be procedural than substantive. First, a freeze may be used to "buy time" by providing an interim response to an immediate economic crisis. Such circumstances have arisen most frequently because of balance-of-payments difficulties or related international monetary problems. The need for some immediate response to the crisis will be especially insistent when the national economy is highly dependent upon international trade. This consideration helps to explain the frequent resort to a freeze in England and the Scandinavian countries.

Second, a wage-price freeze can help to prevent the development of inequities that make it difficult to establish or sustain a more sophisticated form of incomes policy. Although the timing of any incomes policy may be a surprise, government intervention in wage and price decisions seldom

9. Organisation for Economic Cooperation and Development, *Economic Surveys by the OECD: Sweden* (Paris, 1970), p. 12.

takes place in a vacuum. Public discussion of the problem of inflation or hints of crisis often create the expectation that the government will take some decisive action to deal with the situation. During the period preceding the government intervention, some businessmen will raise prices in anticipation of governmental restraints. In contrast, immediate wage increases may be limited by fixed-term collective bargaining agreements and employers' incentives to control costs. If, as a result, price increases sharply outrun wage gains, then when some long-range form of controls is imposed, labor is left with a deep sense of grievance and will press for "catch up" increases that exceed the standard calculated to restore stability. A sudden short-term freeze can prevent this exigency by thwarting anticipatory price increases and preserving the existing relationship between prices and wages.

The failure to impose a freeze or some related measure partially undermined efforts to establish an effective program of control in the United States during the Korean War. At the outset of the war it was apparent that some form of controls would be initiated, but no steps were taken immediately. Prices rose sharply in the last half of 1950 without commensurate wage increases. When economic controls were ordered in early 1951, organized labor expressed a deep sense of inequity that was reflected in the subsequent course of events.[10]

Third, the period of a wage-price freeze can be used to build the national consensus that is necessary to support a durable form of incomes policy. Government leaders can determine the attitudes of the major economic interest groups toward a program of restraint and obtain agreements to cooperate. The stabilization program can be explained to the public at large and modified in the light of the reactions. Initial steps also may be taken during the freeze to build the appropriate administrative machinery so that start-up problems are minimized. Without these preliminaries, any effort to implement an incomes policy is likely to be marked by more than the usual amounts of controversy and inefficiency.

In general, a wage-price freeze is a relatively crude form of economic

10. Between June 1950 and January 1951 the consumer price index rose 6.6 percent and the wholesale price index by 14.5 percent. Mandatory controls were not established until January 25, 1951. The representatives of organized labor walked off the Wage Stabilization Board on February 15, 1951, in a controversy over the appropriate policy governing cost-of-living "catch up." See Milton Derber, "The Wage Stabilization in Historical Perspective," *Proceedings of the Spring Meeting of the Industrial Relations Research Association* (May 1972).

policy. It does not attempt to deal with the subtleties of wage and price adjustments or the complex factors that underlie inflation. In every instance when a wage-price freeze has been imposed—including the events of August 15, 1971—this decision has reflected short-term tactical and political needs and has served as the prelude to more refined policies. A freeze affords time to build a consensus and minimize the sense of inequity on the part of major economic groups while signaling an intention to restore price stability. As a form of incomes policy, a wage-price freeze properly belongs to an opening phase, the time of the sounding of the trumpets rather than the execution of a victorious plan of battle.

III

The Administrative Machinery: Structure and Improvisation

When the President announced the wage-price freeze on the evening of August 15, 1971, only the barest consideration had been given to the bureaucratic machinery that would be necessary to implement the program. The planning for the freeze had been general in nature and was carried out under extreme time limitations. In addition, the secrecy that cloaked the policy discussions meant that it was infeasible to extend the planning process to the working levels of the bureaucracy where detailed blueprints could be drawn. Only three high-level civil servants were involved in the development of options concerning the freeze prior to August 15—and they were not certain whether the exercise had any immediacy or was merely one of the interminable planning efforts that are characteristic of government.

The most pressing requirement was for a bureaucratic mechanism that could become operational without delay. Also, because the freeze was to last only 90 days and the structure of the longer-term stabilization program to follow it was not known at the time, no extended commitments could be made. These circumstances meant that primary responsibility for the conduct of the freeze would have to be assigned to an existing agency of government. There were no obvious candidates for the job. Most of the domestic departments were oriented to particular constituencies and therefore were inappropriate for a task that involved regulating all sectors of the economy. Similarly, the special competence necessary for the efficient administration of the freeze was not lodged in any single agency.

Once an assignment of responsibility was made in the days ahead, the designated agency would need the capacity to respond quickly to the innumerable problems that were likely to arise. Only meager substantive guidance was provided by the terms of the Economic Stabilization Act and the executive order that imposed the freeze. Thus the bureaucratic machinery developed to implement the program would have wide responsibilities ranging from policy formulation and interpretation to public information and compliance. Standard operating procedures clearly would not suffice.

The organization selected would also require an extensive field capability outside of Washington, D.C. Although the President had indicated that the enforcement of the freeze would depend primarily on voluntary compliance, local offices were necessary to provide information and service to the public and to follow up on complaints and violations. To be effective, the agency charged with the conduct of the freeze had to show a flag and not merely sound a distant trumpet.

These structural and operational conditions were subject to the overall Presidential admonition that the freeze should not lay the foundation for a new, massive bureaucracy. In his August 15 speech the President flatly announced: "While the wage-price freeze will be backed by Government sanctions, if necessary, it will not be accompanied by the establishment of a huge price control bureaucracy."[1]

One additional condition was tacitly accepted in developing the administrative machinery for the freeze. Although the decision to impose controls was a dramatic and highly visible Presidential initiative, it was recognized that the President himself should be insulated from the day-to-day operation of the program. On the one hand, it was inappropriate to identify the prestige of the Presidency with inelegant decisions such as determining when an agricultural product was "processed" rather than "raw." On the other hand, there was instinctive recognition that popular support for the freeze was likely to diminish as decisions were made that would impose costs on different segments of society or give rise to allegations of inequity. Accordingly, the administration deemed it important to keep the office of the President removed from actual operations to minimize the political costs of the program to the President in both his personal and institutional capacities. Indeed, at a very early stage of the freeze the President personally indicated his desire to remain completely aloof from the specific decisions or administrative measures. This preference was rigidly adhered to throughout the 90-day period, and on no occasion did the President or his immediate staff intrude upon or exercise influence over the day-to-day operations of the program.[2]

1. "The Challenge of Peace," text of the President's August 15, 1971, radio and television address, *Weekly Compilation of Presidential Documents*, Vol. 7 (August 23, 1971), p. 1170.
2. A week after the freeze had commenced, the President met with top officials concerned with the administration of the program. As the broad coverage of the

The Development of the Administrative Structure

The various operational, tactical, and political requirements were translated into a structure that was a patchwork of new and existing units tied together by a sense of urgency, high-level concern, and the rewards of transient glory. The newly established Cost of Living Council (CLC) stood at the apex of the structure. The formation of CLC originally was proposed in the OMB planning memorandum discussed at the Camp David meeting. It was designed as a Cabinet-level group comprised of the Secretary of the Treasury, the Secretary of Labor, the Secretary of Commerce, the Director of the Office of Emergency Preparedness, the Director of the Office of Management and Budget, and the Chairman of the Council of Economic Advisers. At the Camp David meeting, the working group on wage-price controls enlarged the council to include the Secretary of Agriculture and the President's Special Assistant for Consumer Affairs. In addition, the Chairman of the Board of Governors of the Federal Reserve System was designated as an adviser to the council. This designation of the Chairman of the FRB as an adviser was viewed as highly advantageous to the program and the administration. He had been a vocal advocate of incomes policies. His direct involvement in the program was likely to dampen Congressional criticism while adding his considerable skills as an economist to the process of policy formulation. The Secretary of Housing and Urban Development was added to the council during the first week of the freeze because of his obvious interest in the nature and impact of rent controls.[3]

---

freeze was outlined to him, he asked whether professional football players' salaries were subject to controls. When he was told that they were, he expressed surprise and asked whether this step was necessary in view of the negligible impact of such salaries on the economy and the short average playing life of the professional athlete. The officials replied that it was important to control the players' salaries because of their great visibility and the need to assure the public that the program was being uniformly applied. The President thought a moment and said, "I guess you're right. But whatever you decide, leave me out of it."

3. The following individuals were members of the Cost of Living Council: Secretary of the Treasury John B. Connally (chairman); Paul W. McCracken, Chairman of the Council of Economic Advisers (vice-chairman); George P. Shultz, Director of the Office of Management and Budget; George A. Lincoln, Director of the Office of Emergency Preparedness; Virginia H. Knauer, Special Assistant to the President for Consumer Affairs; Secretary of Agriculture Clifford M. Hardin; Secretary of Labor James D. Hodgson; Secretary of Commerce Maurice H. Stans;

The Cost of Living Council was given three major functions. First, it had final authority for the formulation of specific policies governing the freeze. Second, it had ultimate responsibility for the effective administration of the program although specific functions were delegated to other agencies. Third, CLC was called upon to develop recommendations for the President concerning the post-freeze stabilization program.

Though CLC appeared to be unwieldy at first glance, its composition and functions reflected several conscious considerations. Inclusion of those Cabinet officers with specific constituent groups, such as labor, business, and agriculture, afforded these interests a channel of communication to the process of policy formulation. At the same time, the likelihood that any particular interest would prevail was minimized because of the presence of representatives of competing interests on the council. Moreover, the constituency-oriented members were balanced by the President's principal advisers on economic matters. Overall, the membership of CLC was sufficiently prestigious so that it could exercise maximum leverage throughout the federal establishment but at the same time insulate the President from direct involvement in the program.

CLC had its own staff headed by a full-time Executive Director who also served as Special Assistant to the President. The staff developed policy issues for the council's consideration, supervised the general administration of the program, handled public and Congressional relations, and conducted analytical studies as part of the planning process for the post-freeze stabilization program. The staff was comprised exclusively of persons assigned from other agencies of government. A total of 51 persons served on the CLC staff sometime during the freeze; however, the number never exceeded 45 persons at any one time.

Once it was determined that the Cabinet-level Cost of Living Council should be created to oversee the freeze, the White House cast about for an agency to assume operational responsibility for the program in the field. The President's advisers found the appropriate candidate in the attic of the White House itself—in the form of the Office of Emergency Preparedness. OEP was a relatively obscure agency that had retained a shaky foothold in the Executive Office of the President. It was a redesignation of the Office of Emergency Planning, which had evolved from various "mobiliza-

---

Secretary of Housing and Urban Development George Romney; Arthur F. Burns, Chairman of the Board of Governors of the Federal Reserve System (special adviser to the council).

tion" offices established during the 1950s when concern over nuclear attack was most manifest in the United States. Its primary mission was to develop policies and plans to provide for the continuity of civil government in the event of nuclear war. As anxiety over the prospect of an all-out nuclear war subsided, OEP paid increased attention to related activities such as administering the national stockpile of strategic materials. It also was given responsibility for coordinating relief and assistance in the event of floods, earthquakes, and other natural disasters. Thus OEP had only sporadically come to the public's attention, usually under circumstances of controversy, as when it announced oil import quotas, or calamity, as when it provided aid in the wake of Hurricane Camille which had devastated the Gulf Coast of Mississippi.

At the beginning of the freeze, OEP had a staff of approximately 300 persons: 230 in Washington, D.C., and 70 in 8 regional offices. The agency was headed by George A. Lincoln, a retired army general who had spent 22 years as a professor of economics at West Point. Ironically, the administration currently had under serious consideration a recommendation of the President's Advisory Council on Executive Reorganization (the Ash Council) calling for the abolition of OEP and the distribution of its functions to other agencies.[4]

OEP was selected as the operational arm for the program of economic controls because of its special attributes. As part of its national emergency functions, OEP was responsible for developing economic stabilization plans. Even though this responsibility was carried out on a full-time basis by only one senior civil servant, OEP was the sole agency of government with a bureaucratic commitment to this area.

OEP also had the capacity to act quickly and to mobilize the resources of other government agencies. This skill in mounting a quick response to emergencies reflected OEP's considerable experience in dealing with natural disasters. In addition, it maintained an updated roster of personnel in other government agencies who could be assigned immediately to duties in a stabilization program.

Better yet, despite its small size OEP did have a national field structure

4. On January 26, 1973, President Nixon submitted Reorganization Plan No. 1 of 1973 to Congress, abolishing OEP and transferring most of its functions to other agencies. "The President's Message to the Congress Transmitting Reorganization Plan No. 1 of 1973," *Weekly Compilation of Presidential Documents,* Vol. 9 (January 29, 1973), pp. 76–77.

in all parts of the country. An important element of this structure was a sophisticated, computer-assisted communications network which could be used to disseminate policies and regulations to the field and to provide rapid feedback to Washington.[5]

OEP's involvement in the freeze was determined at the Camp David meeting. George Lincoln was informed of this decision and subsequently played a major role in the planning and the implementation of the program. However, OEP staff both in Washington and in the field were not told of their new assignment until immediately after the President's speech on the evening of August 15. Cost of Living Council Order No. 1, issued on August 17, formally delegated to the Director of OEP "responsibility and authority to implement, administer, monitor, and enforce the stabilization of prices, rents, wages, and salaries. . . ." The order further specified that significant policy decisions should be made only after consultation with the CLC.

The first few days' experience with the freeze clearly indicated that the demands of the program would overwhelm the limited resources of OEP. If the OEP staff members were cast in the role of bureaucratic Spartans, it was apparent that they would be vanquished by the Persians. It was essential to buttress the OEP with other, more extensive, resources so that this agency could give greater attention to operational control and coordination while the informational and compliance functions were carried out by other units.

An immediate review was made of the alternatives available in the federal government. Consideration was given to the feasibility of enlisting the resources of the Internal Revenue Service, the Social Security Administration, the Small Business Administration, and even the Federal Aviation Administration. Although the possibility of utilizing the Social Security Administration had some attraction, it was apparent that the best choice was the IRS. The IRS network of 360 district and subdistrict offices reached into every major metropolitan area and many outlying districts of the country. It had a recognized competence in dealing with the public and communicating otherwise complex rules and regulations in a relatively simple manner. Also, the highly visible enforcement capability of the IRS

5. For a detailed discussion of the role of OEP in the administration of the wage-price freeze, see Harry B. Yoshpe and others, *Stemming Inflation: The Office of Emergency Preparedness and the 90-Day Freeze* (GPO, 1972).

could have significant spillover effects from taxes to wages and prices. Moreover, the fact that IRS was part of the Department of the Treasury and the Secretary of the Treasury was chairman of CLC would simplify bureaucratic problems in retaining IRS's commitment to the program. Beyond these factors, IRS had a reputation as a highly efficient organization, and the timing of the freeze was such that the agency could give substantial resources to the stabilization program without undermining significantly its primary responsibility for tax collection.

With the support of the Secretary of the Treasury, the IRS was formally brought into the stabilization system on August 19. The Deputy Commissioner was made responsible for carrying out those IRS functions directly related to the freeze. The IRS units gave emphasis to informational and compliance activities. Coordination between IRS and OEP was the concern of the Cost of Living Council.

The number of IRS personnel directly involved in the freeze was never known with precision. The agency made extensive use of its taxpayer assistance units in the district and subdistrict offices. In many cases, IRS personnel were assigned to the program as required by the current work load. The best estimate is that during the freeze the equivalent of approximately 2,000 full-time workers were used by IRS in support of the stabilization program.

One additional gap had to be filled to complete the organizational structure. Although IRS had wide coverage, most of its offices were in urban areas. It was necessary to augment this capability with some points of contact that reached into rural areas. To fill this gap, CLC called upon the Agricultural Stabilization and Conservation Service. The ASCS's normal duties included the administration of the various commodity control and credit programs under the Department of Agriculture. Each of the agency's 2,850 county offices was designated as an information center. To each resident county agent went a regulations manual and a set of questions and answers that would permit him to provide information to his constituents. The county agents were further authorized to accept complaints of violations that would be conveyed to the nearest IRS office for action. As the program developed, the ASCS played only a limited role in the administration of the freeze. However, the use of this agency permitted the administration to declare ten days after the commencement of the freeze that the program had comprehensive coverage throughout the country. The linking together of CLC, OEP, IRS, and ASCS constituted an act of bureaucratic improvisation that would have to prevail for the duration of the program.

Making the Program Work

Even before the orders creating this patchwork of bureaucratic responsibilities were issued, the structure had to function at a high level of intensity, if not efficiency. The most pressing requirement was the need for policy guidance. Within minutes after the President concluded his address to the nation on August 15, a flood of inquiries from both governmental agencies and the public had to be answered. Once policies were formulated, procedures had to be established for their dissemination and subsequent interpretations and rulings. And because the wage-price freeze was essentially a regulatory process, a system had to be devised to provide for exemptions and compliance.

Policy Formulation

The first steps at policy formulation were taken by a small, ad hoc group late in the evening of August 15. The members of this group were the Chairman of the Council of Economic Advisers, the Director of OEP, the newly designated Executive Director of the Cost of Living Council, and related staff personnel. Guided by little more than an appreciation of the objectives of the President's program and an intuitive sense of the issues that required immediate attention, this group provided preliminary policy recommendations concerning a wide variety of issues such as the applicability of the freeze to prospective increases in college tuition and the status of state and local government employees. This ad hoc group was quickly supplanted as the major policy forum by the full Cost of Living Council. CLC held its first meeting on Tuesday, August 17, and met virtually every weekday thereafter for the next month.

The initial determinations of CLC in the policy area were sporadic and poorly prepared because of staff limitations and the general confusion associated with the early stages of the program. In a perverse manner, the internal process of policy formulation reflected the public relations requirements of the program. On the very first day a question-and-answer format was adopted to provide guidance to the public concerning the rules governing the freeze. Hence, at the first few meetings of the Cost of Living Council, the text discussed was generally a set of proposed questions and answers. A typical item up for consideration might read:

Q. Are deferred increases under the terms of existing labor agreements covered by the freeze?

A. Yes.

This approach suited the immediate informational needs of the public better than it did the analytical demands posed by major policy issues. The question-and-answer format did not lend itself to the identification of alternatives or the intensive examination of the implications of the various policy options. Nonetheless, this approach did offer a vehicle for quickly establishing major policies and conveying them to the public.

Within the first week, an alternative procedure for policy formulation was developed which functioned more or less without change for the duration of the freeze. Initial responsibility for the identification of issues for possible review by CLC was delegated to OEP and a small policy review staff of the council. OEP was the primary channel for the identification and analysis of issues generated by public inquiries. When IRS received a request for guidance or information that could not be satisfied because of gaps or ambiguities in existing policies, the matter was referred to the closest OEP regional office. If the regional specialists could not provide an adequate response, the matter was brought to the attention of the OEP national office. The issue was subject to further review by a small "resource analysis" staff. Those issues that were still unresolved were referred to the Executive Policy Committee (EPC) of the Cost of Living Council.

The Executive Policy Committee was set up to make definitive interpretations of existing policies and to provide recommendations of new policies to the full council. It was comprised of the Chairman of CEA, who served as chairman of the committee, the Executive Director of CLC, the Director of OEP, and the Under Secretary of the Treasury.[6] The EPC met on a daily basis and reviewed the issues that were brought to it for consideration by OEP and CLC staff. OEP would "batch" individual inquiries or

6. The members of the Executive Policy Committee were; Paul W. McCracken, Chairman of the Council of Economic Advisers (chairman); George A. Lincoln, Director of the Office of Emergency Preparedness; Charls E. Walker, Under Secretary of the Treasury; and myself, Arnold R. Weber, Executive Director of the Cost of Living Council. The leading staff personnel were: Edgar R. Fiedler, Cost of Living Council; Earl D. Rhode, Cost of Living Council; and Louis Neeb, Office of Emergency Preparedness.

issues so that they were presented to the Executive Policy Committee in their most general form. In addition, CLC staff would review the policy issue so that explicit consideration was given to the impact of any narrow decision on related policies. The EPC would then make a determination on the basis of existing policy that would become an authoritative ruling of CLC and OEP. In other cases, the EPC would conclude that the issue presented was not covered by existing policies and would require action by the full council. A recommendation would be drafted and the issue would be brought to CLC as expeditiously as possible.

As the freeze progressed, the EPC became the most important unit in the organizational structure. First, it convened regularly, and the sessions lasted as long as was necessary to complete the business at hand. Second, it interpreted many of the general policies that had been enunciated by the council. For example, CLC had ruled that individual workers who had completed a bona fide training program could receive wage increases without being in violation of the freeze. The precise criteria governing the definition of an acceptable training program were left to EPC. Third, by selecting those issues that would go to the council and by making recommendations concerning the disposition of these issues, EPC clearly exercised great influence in the process of policy formulation. It was for this reason that EPC was informally dubbed "the Committee on Public Safety." Clearly the EPC exercised extraordinary powers over the conduct of the freeze and hence the operation of the economy. Either comfort or concern may be drawn from the fact that all four principals on the committee had an extensive academic background in economics.

Despite the fact that the Executive Policy Committee came to play a key role in the process of policy formulation, the Cost of Living Council remained an active forum for discussion and decision making throughout the freeze. The usual experience with large, Cabinet-level groups indicated that the effectiveness of CLC would rapidly diminish because of the inability or unwillingness of the individual members to spend the required time. Because of the great prominence of the program, however, particularly in the early stages, the various Cabinet officers maintained a high level of participation.

Over the course of the freeze CLC acted upon about 75 major policy issues. These issues collectively touched every aspect of the program's operation. The normal procedure followed during the council meetings was to review a staff paper analyzing an issue under consideration. Normally, the staff paper provided a range of options and a recommended course of action from the Executive Policy Committee. After discussion, the council might accept the recommendation of EPC, accept it with modifications, reject it, or call for additional analysis. In fact, the council rejected or modified staff recommendations for about one-fifth of the issues presented for decision.

In general, the council operated through consensus rather than formal votes. On a few occasions, differences in points of view were so entrenched that formal votes were taken. Beneath the customary consensus, however, certain persistent differences in approach characterized the operation of the council. There was a significant divergence between those members who represented departments with explicit constituencies and those who headed central agencies of government with broader responsibilities. The Cabinet officers from constituent-oriented agencies such as Commerce, Agriculture, and Labor were disposed to approach an issue from the vantage point of their special interests. They espoused "understanding" in resolving issues that had a direct impact on their constituents, while the members from the central agencies adopted a relatively inflexible position when handling issues that would affect the credibility or rigor of the stabilization program.

As the council operated, special interests were seldom accommodated; indeed, where they were raised, a more restrictive policy might be adopted. Despite the protests of the Secretary of Agriculture, ceiling prices were imposed on the sale of stumpage by the Forest Service even though stumpage might have qualified for an exemption as a "raw agricultural product." Similarly, the council rejected a request by the Secretary of Labor to provide some assurance to the bituminous coal mine operators that the cost of any labor agreement could be passed on in the form of higher prices. The Secretary of Labor had requested this assurance in order to facilitate the settlement of a strike involving the United Mine Workers and the bituminous coal operators. And the Secretary of Commerce was virtually directed to undertake intensive jawboning against those firms that had increased their dividends in violation of the program of voluntary compliance initiated by the council.

In each case, those council members who regarded the issue from a White House vantage point or from the point of view of a central agency of government exerted pressure for a tough position. In addition, any individual council member espousing a view that would favor his constituents was likely to be neutralized by a council member seeking to protect a constituency with conflicting interests.

Another underlying source of controversy within the council was the different philosophies of what might be characterized as the hardliners and the softliners. Among the council members there were perceptible differences of opinion concerning the scope and degree of stringency with which the freeze should be administered. These differences might have been ideological in origin, but they tended to be expressed within the framework of specific issues. Those council members with a less rigorous approach to the freeze generally favored wider exemptions, some pass-through of costs, and a flexible attitude toward the operation of existing contract provisions that might result in increases in wages. It is accurate to say that, overall, the hardline position prevailed and that marginal issues were generally decided in favor of restraint and "toughness" rather than flexibility.

Although CLC performed with considerable harmony and efficiency as a decision-making body for Phase I, it was less effective in reaching agreement on the principles and details that were to govern the post-freeze stabilization program. The issues involved were too complex for so large a group, and the interests of the members were too diverse to reach agreement without the development of explicit coalitions and the willingness to override the vigorous opposition of particular members. Because the council, in a large degree, functioned as a collegial body, it was not geared to handle issues which posed difficult internal political problems. Consequently, the Cost of Living Council defined the general issues and options involved in planning for Phase II, but the basic decisions ultimately were made by the President in concert with his chief economic advisers.

Administration and Coordination

Once the policies governing the freeze were formulated, quick action was necessary to insure that they were conveyed rapidly to the public and throughout the field structure. In addition, interpretations and rulings on the general policies had to be made while steps were taken to insure compliance or at least to maintain the symbols of compliance.

The general policies were translated into operational rules through two means. As noted previously, extensive use was made of the question-and-answer technique. Although this approach had a synthetic quality, it proved to be extremely effective with the press and other media, and the "official" questions and answers were periodically incorporated in booklets and comprehensive summaries. Yet, since the questions and answers did not constitute official rulings, they could not be used as the basis for legal enforcement. Indeed, where adversary proceedings developed, apparent ambiguities or inconsistencies in the questions and answers were used as a defense against legal action concerning alleged violations of the freeze. This problem arose particularly in dealing with the question of teachers' salaries. In this case, the major teacher organizations attempted to demonstrate that the questions and answers providing guidance on this issue were sufficiently misleading or inconsistent as to justify the payment of previously scheduled salary increases.[7] Nonetheless, the question-and-answer technique was an extremely useful device for the widespread dissemination of relatively simple statements of policy in a short period of time.

For enforcement purposes, the specific policies also had to be translated into formal regulations for publication in the *Federal Register*. With the publication of these regulations, they acquired legal standing and became enforceable. In accordance with the provisions of the Administrative Procedure Act, there is generally a time lag between the publication of regulations in the *Federal Register* and their effective date. In the intervening period, interested parties are given time to criticize or otherwise comment on the proposed regulations before they are put in their final form. With regard to the freeze, however, the prior notice period was waived. This waiver was made in accordance with a general escape clause in the Administrative Procedure Act to accommodate emergency situations. Although this abbreviated procedure clearly did violence to due process in matters of enormous importance to various sectors of the economy, it was justified on the grounds that prior notification and hearings would so delay the promulgation of final rules that the wage-price freeze would be reduced to a nullity.

Once the regulations were published, primary responsibility for providing information to the public and rendering interpretation was assumed by IRS and OEP. After the first few weeks of the freeze, the local IRS offices constituted the initial contact with the public. In general, IRS did a satisfactory job of providing simplified guidance on the most recurrent questions. Nonetheless, there was a continuing problem of consistency of guidance among the various IRS offices. In many instances, different IRS offices would provide different answers to the same questions—an incon-

7. This argument was persuasive to the court in *United States* v. *Jefferson Parish School Board*, 333 F. Supp. 418 (E.D. La. 1971).

sistency that was revealed in a somewhat overdramatized manner by the more enterprising newspapers. In order to minimize the possible inconsistencies of response, a detailed manual was provided for IRS offices. The problem was a substantial one throughout the course of the freeze, however, and reflected the lack of adequate training of many of the IRS local office personnel who were diverted from their normal duties and pressed into service on extremely short notice.

The more difficult or highly technical questions of interpretation were referred to the OEP regional and national staff and the policy review unit of the Cost of Living Council. These units were asked to determine when honey was transformed from a raw to a processed agricultural product, whether the "seasonality rule" applied to Halloween candy, and the status of commercial rental leases whereby the amount of rent was determined by volume of sales of the retail occupant. Each of the issues was "staffed out" in some detail. In many instances, specialized expertise was called upon from other departments of government. Ultimately, about 400 of these issues reached the Executive Policy Committee for resolution or further referral to CLC. OEP headquarters' staff was responsible for "batching" the issues and insuring that they reached the EPC in a timely manner.

Early in the program it was recognized that extreme caution had to be exercised in developing a general principle from the details of a specific case. Instead, the implications of an individual ruling were carefully explored before a general policy was formulated. For example, during the first days of the freeze a ruling was made permitting previously scheduled college tuition increases to go into effect. Because this narrow question was resolved without reference to the more general issue concerning the status of futures contracts of all kinds, the tuition rule turned out to be inconsistent with the rules later applied to analogous situations. Considerable intellectual and bureaucratic energy was subsequently expended to provide an ex post rationalization for the difference in treatment.

The granting of exceptions and individual exemptions to existing rules and regulations was closely held by the Cost of Living Council itself. In view of the great concern over the need for maintaining a uniform, stringent approach to the freeze, no exception could be granted without the approval of CLC. Approximately ten requests for exceptions were brought to the full council. The basic policy decision revolved around the extent to which impending business bankruptcy would be taken into account in granting an exception or exemption from the freeze. CLC ruled that impending bankruptcy, by itself, was not a sufficient basis for setting aside the existing restraints. Once this policy and related issues of a less portentous nature were determined, some authority for handling exemptions was shifted to the field. The field offices, however, were clearly sensitive to the cues that had been transmitted, and in no instance did they provide for an exception.

The administration of compliance activities posed the most complex administrative problem during the course of the freeze. This complexity arose from the distribution of functions among the operating agencies and the authority relationships between the various levels of the hastily improvised organizational structure. Initial responsibility for securing compliance resided with Internal Revenue. IRS was obliged to follow up on any complaint and, through autonomous actions of its field staff, to identify violations. When compliance was not forthcoming on the basis of informal discussions between IRS and the alleged violator, IRS initiated a full investigation with the objective of providing the facts and related documentation necessary for legal proceedings. This file was then referred to the OEP regional office. The OEP regional director reviewed the file in conjunction with the U.S. Assistant Attorney assigned by the Justice Department. If they were unable to obtain compliance or close the case by a ruling of "no violation," the matter was then conveyed to Washington.

At each point in this process sharp differences in opinion might develop among IRS, OEP, and the Justice Department. On several occasions, individual decisions to litigate an alleged violation were made only after prolonged discussions involving the Director of OEP, the Executive Director of CLC, and the Assistant Attorney-General of the Civil Division. The latter agency handles most litigation for the government and is highly protective of this prerogative. The administrative system for compliance activities never functioned smoothly during the freeze despite some progress in dissipating bureaucratic conflicts.

The administrative structure established to carry out the freeze suffered from obvious deficiencies. There was a wide diffusion of authority, communications were often sporadic and complicated by the involvement of many different agencies, and the continual need to provide effective coordination was acute. Nonetheless, on balance, the performance of this improvised structure was adequate to the task and outstanding in the light of the extreme demands that were placed on it under such short notice.

The effectiveness of the administrative structure was abetted by several fortuitous factors. The availability of OEP in the Executive Office of the President provided a highly versatile resource with the capacity for quick reactions. The fact that the freeze was instituted in August, during IRS's "off season," permitted the conscription of a significant share of that agency's staff without unduly impairing its primary mission. And the participation of many Cabinet-level departments in the CLC created an implicit commitment to discard normal bureaucratic restrictions in providing service to the program.

Above all, however, the system worked because the task generated a sense of importance and dedication that is rare in large bureaucracies. Essentially, the administrative system did the job because it was not ensnared in procedures that often constrain normal governmental activities. The structure that was designed would have proven too cumbersome and diffuse to operate effectively over a long period. But for a 90-day effort it provided a vehicle for the rapid mobilization of resources, flexibility in the use of these resources, and the application of considerable intelligence and dedication.

IV

Defining the Freeze:
The Question of Coverage

The wide coverage of the freeze was designed to have a shock effect on expectations and to complement the other sweeping elements of the administration's shift in economic policy. No systematic effort was made to relate the scope of the freeze to an underlying economic theory or to the complexities of intersectoral relationships. The fact that the freeze was imposed as a short-term policy to be succeeded by a more discriminating system of controls also implied that it was preferable to err on the side of universality of coverage rather than restraint. Any economic distortions or inequities created by the blanket coverage were viewed as transient consequences that would be justified by the shock effect of the freeze. As individual questions of coverage arose, they were resolved by a series of tactical judgments made in the light of the overall objectives of the freeze and the terms of the statutory authority.

The provisions of the Economic Stabilization Act of 1970, as amended, provided for the inclusion of most forms of income and prices within the scope of the freeze. The act empowered the President "to issue such orders and regulations as he may deem appropriate to stabilize prices, rents, wages, and salaries. . . ."[1] The act did not include any criteria for identifying industries in which price and wage increases had been excessive or "unstabilizing." Nor was the President given significant discretion to tailor coverage to those sectors of the economy that might most affect the overall price level.

To the contrary, when the act was extended in May 1971, an amendment was added that virtually dictated comprehensive coverage. Shortly before the original act was scheduled to expire, the President had used it as his authority for imposing a program of wage restraint on the construction industry. Congress reacted by amending the act to delimit carefully the circumstances under which the President could exercise selective restraints.

1. P.L. 91-379 (August 15, 1970), sec. 202.

The criteria were so proscriptive that they made it difficult for the President to select any option other than the across-the-board application of controls. The amendment read:

(b) The authority conferred on the President by this section shall not be exercised with respect to a particular industry or segment of the economy unless the President determines, after taking into account the seasonal nature of employment, the rate of employment or underemployment, and other mitigating factors, that prices or wages in that industry or segment of the economy have increased at a rate which is grossly disproportionate to the rate at which prices or wages have increased in the economy generally.[2]

The terms of the statute were also significant for the forms of income that were excluded from the President's regulatory authority. The act was silent on whether the President could take steps to control profits, interest, and dividends. The prudent interpretation of this omission was to assume that the Congress did not intend to extend controls to these forms of income even though there was a loud clamor for their inclusion in the freeze. Some Congressmen pressed for the inclusion of interest as the "price" of borrowing money. It was unreasonable, however, to interpret the term "prices" in the generic sense. If this had been the intent of Congress, it was illogical to single out rents, wages, and salaries but not other "prices." In addition, there had been an effort to expand the coverage of the act to include interest specifically, but it had been beaten back in the Congress.

The statutory pressures for comprehensive coverage of prices, rents, wages, and salaries clearly would create administrative problems, but the difficulties were not considered to be insuperable. To be sure, the President had expressed his distaste for a "huge bureaucracy" to administer the program of controls. Presumably, the more comprehensive the coverage, the larger the bureaucracy that would be required to administer the program. But it was believed that a cumbersome bureaucracy could be avoided by arousing public support for the program and by appealing for voluntary compliance. Any anxiety over the imbalance between the coverage of the freeze and the administrative mechanisms established to implement the program were outweighed by a concern for equity. And equity was initially achieved by expanding coverage as broadly as possible even though the consequences might be economically deleterious or frivolous. Where exemptions were made, they were directly supportive of the overall goals of the President's program, were necessary to sustain *other* governmental

2. P.L. 92-15 (May 18, 1971), sec. 3.

programs, or were justified by reference to experience in previous episodes of wage-price control.

Within this framework, the determination of the coverage of the wage-price freeze went forward at three levels. First, it was necessary to decide the broad scope of the freeze with respect to major forms of income. Second, judgments had to be made concerning the inclusion of particular sectors of the economy. Third, a series of technical judgments had to be made to determine whether certain kinds of transactions fell within the definition of wages and prices and hence were covered by the freeze.

Extending the Freeze

It was taken for granted that the freeze would include those forms of income spelled out by the statute—i.e., wages, salaries, prices, and rent. From this starting point the Cost of Living Council deliberated the question of what steps, if any, should be taken by legal or extralegal measures to extend the program of restraint to profits, interest, and dividends. The idea of controlling profits was quickly rejected. Any effort to determine actual profits for the 90-day period would require tenuous accounting judgments and probably was infeasible. It was also argued that pressure would be exerted on profits by maintaining a rigid policy with respect to prices. To be sure, particular firms might enjoy windfall profits because of large fluctuations in volume, productivity increases, or other special circumstances, but such profits could be viewed as a consequence of the random incidence of gains and losses that arose from the timing of the freeze.

Beyond these factors, the Cost of Living Council was reluctant to control profits at a time when a creditable case could be made that they were already at a relatively low level.[3] Despite vociferous complaints made by

3. Between 1966 and 1970 the ratio of corporation profits for all industries (before taxes and with inventory valuation adjustment) to gross national private product had declined significantly. The ratios between 1964 and 1971 were:

1964	11.6	1968	10.9
1965	12.3	1969	9.5
1966	12.2	1970	8.1
1967	11.1	1971	8.5

Data from U.S. Bureau of Economic Analysis, *Survey of Current Business,* relevant issues.

organized labor and a few other groups, the clamor to "do something" abated when several economists who had been associated with the Kennedy-Johnson administration testified before the Joint Economic Committee in opposition to any direct controls over profits or the enactment of an excess profits tax.[4]

Interest rates were not afforded the same tolerant view as profits. Under the terms of the Credit Control Act of 1969, the President could direct the Chairman of the Board of Governors of the Federal Reserve System to study means to control the use of credit in order to prevent "inflationary spirals." The Federal Reserve Chairman could then recommend to the President specific measures to attain this goal, including the regulation of interest rates.[5] The fact that the Federal Reserve Chairman at that time was a special adviser to the Cost of Living Council gave this alternative a personal element of feasibility. Aside from considerations of equity, the pressure for including interest rates in the program of economic controls was intensified by sharp criticisms from Congressman Wright Patman, the Chairman of the House Banking Committee, who with populist intensity and endurance had been waging a battle against what he considered excessive interest rates.

Ultimately, the Cost of Living Council decided against the imposition of controls over interest rates. The Credit Control Act of 1969 was deemed inapplicable because it was designed to deal with credit shortages, a condition which did not prevail during the freeze. Also, any effort to interpret the Economic Stabilization Act elastically to include interest rates would be illusory because of the provision of the law which stated that the ceiling price for any commodity could not be lower than the price in effect on May 25, 1970. Since interest rates on May 25, 1970, were considerably higher than on August 15, 1971, the application of the freeze to interest rates would have virtually no effect. And last, because one of the primary objectives of the overall program was to dissipate inflationary expectations,

4. See "Statement of Walter Heller," in *The President's New Economic Program,* Hearings before the Joint Economic Committee, 92 Cong. 1 sess. (1971), pp. 14–15. Heller was Chairman of the Council of Economic Advisers during the Kennedy-Johnson administration. Gardner Ackley, another former Chairman of the CEA, also testified against controls on profits (*The President's New Economic Program,* pp. 258–59).

5. P.L. 91-151 (December 23, 1969), secs. 205–6. See *Lowering Interest Rates, Fighting Inflation, Helping Small Business, and Expanding the Mortgage Market,* Conference Report to accompany S. 2577, 91 Cong. 1 sess. (1969).

it was hoped that the freeze itself would lead to a decline in interest rates as a kind of by-product, demonstrating the wisdom of the administration's refusal to take direct measures to control this form of income.[6]

These considerations persuaded the administration to resort to exhortation rather than formal methods of control. Acting on the request of the Cost of Living Council, the Secretary of the Treasury in a letter to about 40,000 financial institutions requested that they hold the line on interest charges. The question of taking stronger measures was reconsidered several times during the freeze. The discussions focused on the possibility of establishing selective controls over the interest charged for consumer credit. However, the decline in several key interest rates provided the necessary reassurance, and no additional steps were taken. Parenthetically, it may be noted that the Economic Stabilization Act as amended by Congress in December of 1971—during Phase II of the stabilization program —did grant the President the power to control interest rates and further required him to explain to the Congress why this action was not taken in the event that he did not choose to exercise the authority.

The need for symbolic restraint over the activities of the financial community was further satisfied by applying a well-publicized program of jaw-boning in the matter of dividends. In the days immediately following the commencement of the freeze, prices on the stock market rose rapidly, a development which brought forth criticism that while the freeze was holding down the earnings of workers, it was creating windfall profits for stockholders. The reaction to this outcry was to extend the program to dividends. Although the President did not have the authority to control dividends, it was decided to request corporations to limit dividends to the level of the last quarterly payment that had been made before the freeze.[7]

6. In fact, interest rates did generally decline throughout the freeze. The rate on newly issued 90-day government securities fell from 5.078 in August 1971 to 4.191 in November. The yield on Aaa bonds declined from 7.59 in August to 7.26 in November. Meanwhile the prime rate charged by banks dropped from 6 percent in July to 5⅜–5½ percent at the end of the freeze. (Data from *Survey of Current Business,* Vol. 52 [July 1972], and *Federal Reserve Bulletin,* Vol. 58 [January 1972].) Whether the decline in interest rates can be attributed to the freeze is debatable. However, from the point of view of the stabilization program, the important consideration was that the interest rates did decline.

7. The policies concerning dividends became somewhat more complicated than simply limiting payments to the level that had prevailed in the last quarter. Special allowances were made for end-of-year bonuses and payouts mandatory under law. But the basic concept was to apply the same limitations to dividends as to other income shares.

This step was taken with the recognition that it was economically innocuous. Imposing a ceiling on dividend payments would, in some cases, permit a corporation to retain a larger proportion of its earnings. Presumably, this situation would be reflected in an increase in the price of the stock. Moreover, short-term limitations on dividend payments tended to be meaningless because any increase could be shifted to subsequent periods with little difficulty. Nonetheless, largely for symbolic reasons, dividends were subjected to voluntary controls. And unlike the approach taken to interest rates, exhortation was reinforced by an organized program of monitoring dividend payments. When apparent violations of the guidelines were identified, the firms involved were subject to intensive pressure by government officials to rescind their actions.

Significantly, even though the Cost of Living Council extended the spirit, if not the letter, of the stabilization program to almost all forms of income and prices, it resisted the most clamorous demand from the public. Throughout the freeze there was a heavy demand for extending controls to state and local taxes. Undoubtedly, this reflected many individual citizens' view of their economic plight. Especially for homeowners, taxes appeared to be a major, rapidly rising component of the cost of living. Landlords also felt the pinch of higher taxes when it was subsequently ruled that they would not be permitted to pass along tax increases in the form of higher rents. No serious consideration was ever given to the inclusion of state and local taxes in the scope of the freeze, but these demands indicated the intensity of the public pressure for comprehensive economic controls during the period of the freeze.

Exclusion by Sector

Once the basic coverage was determined by reference to forms of income, it was necessary to refine the scope of the program in terms of particular sectors or economic units. Because of the restrictions in the statute and the pressures for universality, these refinements were made by consideration of a series of possible exclusions rather than as an expression of any sophisticated strategy.

The only exclusion made at the outset involved raw (unprocessed) agricultural products. This decision was reached in the prior planning for the freeze and was based on a mixture of historical, administrative, and economic factors. First, raw agricultural products had been excluded from controls during World War II and the Korean War. Second, there were severe doubts that controls could work in the agricultural sector. Even within a 90-day period shortages and black markets could develop as suppliers withheld their products from regular channels of distribution. Third, the administrative burdens of maintaining even a pretense of effective controls on such products were almost insuperable. Literally thousands of products were involved and were subject to day-to-day fluctuations based on local market and seasonal considerations. If raw agricultural products were covered by the freeze, an infinite number of complaints would be forthcoming with little prospect for remedial action. Fourth, supplies of farm products were generally abundant, and the recent trend of prices of raw agricultural products had been relatively stable. Hopefully, these conditions would persist through the freeze period.

Last, many raw agricultural commodities were subject to price support and stabilization programs made mandatory by Congress. The intent of these programs was to maintain or to increase the price of particular commodities such as wheat, feed grains, peanuts, cotton, tobacco, etc. In the event that prices were not permitted to increase, government purchases might be required by law. Hence the inclusion of these products within the scope of the freeze could result in significant market distortions and large costs to the federal government with a commensurate impact on the budget.

The second major category of exclusions involved exports and imports. Although the original executive order was silent on this issue, it had to be resolved quickly in the light of the overall objectives of the administration's altered economic policy. On the one hand, an overriding aim of the policy was to improve the U.S. position in the world markets to provide a stimulus to American production and employment. If the prices of imports were controlled, foreign goods would be able to preserve any existing advantage in American markets. On the other hand, the price of imports could have a significant impact on the consumer price index. Trade considerations prevailed, and imports were exempted from the price freeze. To the extent that import prices did rise, American goods would be in an improved relative position in the domestic market.

The subsequent interpretation of the rules governing imports further strengthened the advantage to American goods. The price of *finished* goods sold directly in the American market could rise without restraint. However, if an imported good was incorporated in another commodity, the increased price could not be reflected in the price of the final product which was still subject to controls. This rule would have the effect of compressing the gross margins of American firms using imported components if the price of the components rose. Since the prices of American-produced components were frozen, there would be some incentive to shift away from imported components, although the likelihood of this adjustment taking place in the short run was slight.

Exports were also excluded from the freeze. The reason for this action was more forthright than in the case of imports. Because export prices did not enter into the domestic cost of living directly, it was considered unnecessary to impose restraints on these transactions. Moreover, the feasibility of determining the prices of transactions abroad was questionable. Some concern was expressed that if the price of certain goods, particularly raw materials, rose in foreign markets, there would be a diversion of domestic supplies to the export trade, raising prices or creating shortages within the United States. Such a sequence of events did take place toward the end of the freeze in the animal hides market. Because Argentina had imposed export controls on hides to offset reductions in cattle slaughter, fewer hides were available for export from that country to foreign markets. Consequently, the world market price rose and caused the diversion of animal hides from the American market to buyers abroad. The general approach of the Cost of Living Council in such circumstances was to permit these reactions to take place on the understanding that if the situation became extreme, the Secretary of Commerce would impose export controls under the authority of existing legislation. This step was never taken during the freeze.

The most significant decision in defining the scope of the wage-price freeze involved the inclusion of state and municipal governments. When Executive Order 11615 promulgated the freeze, it was not clear whether state and municipal governments were covered. State and local governments had been exempt from economic controls in the past, and the authority of the federal government to limit the wage and price decisions of these governmental units was uncertain. Indeed, at the outset of the freeze the Cost of Living Council staff assumed that state and local governments would be exempt. This issue was put in a new context when, shortly after August 15, Governor Preston Smith of Texas announced that he planned to implement a wage and salary increase for state employees. The fact that the Governor chose to make his announcement in a public and somewhat flamboyant manner focused immediate attention on the issue. The fact that within Texas Governor Smith was in the opposite political camp to Secretary Connally gave the matter a personal, political dimension that thrust it into the limelight.

Under conditions of some urgency, the Department of Justice drafted an opinion for the Cost of Living Council declaring that the President had the authority to apply the freeze to state and local governments. The opinion cited the sweeping language of Section 202 of the Economic Stabilization Act which authorized the President to issue "such orders and regulations as he may deem appropriate." Further reference was made to two Supreme Court cases, *Case* v. *Bowles* and *Maryland* v. *Wirtz*. In the former case, the Supreme Court had held that the Emergency Price Control Act of 1942 was constitutional as applied to lumber sales by the state of Washington.[8] In *Maryland* v. *Wirtz,* the Supreme Court held that state employees could be covered by the provisions of the Fair Labor Standards Act.[9]

Armed with this opinion, the council ruled that state and local governments were covered by the stabilization program and made preparations to enforce that decision in the courts. The prospect of a legal test was averted when both the Comptroller and Attorney-General of the state of Texas published statements declaring that, in their judgment, the ban on salary increases for state employees was lawful and would be adhered to. The fact that both of these officials were elected gave them the degree of independence, if not acumen, necessary to reach this conclusion. Governor Smith soon backed down and indicated his willingness to conform to the ruling of the Cost of Living Council. The action precipitated by the Texas case not only resulted in the coverage of state and local government employee wages but also widened the freeze to cover the rates charged for specific services such as sewerage, water, and electricity.

The Texas cause célèbre was closely followed by another dramatic incident, this time involving the Department of Defense. In the first week of the freeze, a spokesman for DOD publicly stated that the department's activities were not bound by the Cost of Living Council's rulings. Again, this statement was viewed as a major challenge to the program. The particular point in conflict was payment of longevity increases and other special allowances to members of the armed forces. Secretary Connally quickly reaffirmed the council's decision that the department was covered by the program and would have to comply. Whatever the merits of the case were, DOD beat a hasty retreat, and Deputy Secretary of Defense David Packard issued a statement indicating that the department would adhere to the regulations of the council.

Once this skirmish was concluded, a whole range of Defense Depart-

8. 327 U.S. 92, 99.
9. 392 U.S. 183.

ment activities became enmeshed in the stabilization program, including the prices charged at military commissaries, educational allowances to personnel abroad, and payments to foreign nationals employed by the Department of Defense. When a bill increasing military pay was passed by Congress in late September 1971, CLC ruled—with the affirmation of the President—that these increases could not become effective until the end of the freeze on November 14, 1971.[10]

Although it lacked the show business aspects of the Texas and Department of Defense incidents, the question of providing an exemption for wage earners with low incomes posed a more substantial question. During World War II and the Korean conflict, a general exemption was provided for wage increases that were necessary to correct "substandards of living." This approach was based on social considerations and was designed to effect a redistribution of income—a collateral goal of wage stabilization programs that has been adopted both in the United States and abroad. At the same time, the Economic Stabilization Act provided for the relief of "gross inequities." Presumably, the existence of "substandards of living" could be interpreted to constitute a "gross inequity."

The question of providing an exemption for workers with substandard income arose as an aftermath of the Texas case. Following the acquiescence of Governor Smith to the Cost of Living Council ruling, an association of public employees in Texas petitioned for relief from the freeze on the grounds that the income of many of its members fell below the poverty line. This issue was discussed at some length by the council, and it was decided that such an exemption should not be provided during the freeze.

The reasons for rejecting the petition touched upon various philosophical considerations underlying the freeze. A number of policy makers maintained that the wage-price freeze was not intended to be a social program with redistributive goals. Although the abolition of poverty was a laudable objective of the government, it could best be achieved through other programs. In addition, there was some concern that public support for the program would be eroded by an exemption on social grounds. And once wages were allowed to rise in order to accommodate a poverty criterion, pressure would be exerted to permit pass-through of these increases in costs to the price charged. For these reasons, the Cost of Living Council

10. P.L. 92-129 (September 28, 1971); "Draft Extension and Military Pay Bill," text of the President's September 28, 1971, statement upon signing the bill, *Weekly Compilation of Presidential Documents,* Vol. 7 (October 4, 1971), p. 1355.

rejected the petition with the admonition that the issue would be considered in the post-freeze period. As to general recognition of the needs of poor people, CLC pointed out that welfare payments, food stamps, and other transfer payments had been exempted—since they were not wages—and therefore could be raised. The council also had ruled that increases in wages to comply with federal and state minimum wage laws were permissible under the terms of the freeze.

Adjustments at the Edges

Once the boundaries of the freeze were determined, the Cost of Living Council was obliged to make a series of specific technical judgments which further refined the coverage of the stabilization program. In some cases, the council was able to extricate itself from thickets that had not been foreseen; in other instances, the council was ensnared by the logic of its original determinations which led to frivolous or counter-productive rulings.

One immediate problem was the status of price changes made by American firms that were members of international price-fixing arrangements. In May 1971 the international conference that set maritime shipping rates in the Pacific had agreed to a 17.5 percent increase in the rates charged for the shipment of goods from the Far East to the United States. Scheduled to take effect on October 1, 1971, this increase was designed to narrow the differential that existed between the rates charged for freight leaving the United States and for goods shipped into this country.

For many years, a differential rate structure had existed whereby shipping charges on goods sent from the Far East to the United States were significantly lower than those levied on goods leaving the United States for the Far East. This differential was based on historical considerations and was now viewed as discriminatory to American exporters. The fact that the differential specifically favored the shipment of goods from Japan to the United States heightened governmental concern over the existing rate structure. Consequently, the Federal Maritime Commission (FMC), which has broad responsibilities in this area, had exerted great pressure on the international convention to narrow the differentials. Beginning in 1969, shipping rates on goods moving from the Far East to the United States had been increased three times. The scheduled October 1 increase was part of the continued effort of the FMC to attain equality of freight rates.

Against this background, the Chairman of the FMC, Helen D. Bentley, petitioned the Cost of Living Council to exempt from the freeze increases in freight rates charged by American carriers pursuant to international convention agreements. The narrow issue was the jurisdiction of the council over international shipping rates. The broader issue was the contention that the scheduled increase was consistent with the objectives of the administration's economic program and would strengthen the position of American goods in foreign markets while helping to stem the movement of imports from Japan. The State Department joined the FMC in asserting that any effort to prevent the implementation of the new rates would have a deleterious effect on our relations with the other countries involved. Although the case at hand involved an international shipping conference covering the Pacific routes, the FMC also indicated that a similar submission would be forthcoming from the North Atlantic convention. Here, a cartel arrangement had broken down two years before, leading to sharp rate competition among the shipping companies. The North Atlantic Conference was being reestablished and was expected to promulgate a new, higher schedule of freight rates along the North Atlantic routes from American ports to various European cities.

After prolonged discussion, the Cost of Living Council denied the request for an exemption. Although the scheduled increase in freight rates was viewed as consistent with the overall objectives of the President's economic program, other, short-term considerations prevailed. First, the delay in the introduction of the new rate schedule would last only until the middle of November. It was assumed that any post-freeze price control agency would take a longer view. Second, CLC was reluctant to grant an exemption that would appear to favor business as opposed to other groups in the economy. In particular, if the increase in freight rates brought short-term windfall profits to American shipping firms, the administration might become vulnerable to criticisms from organized labor, whose members had been denied wage increases scheduled to take effect during the freeze. Consistent with its acceptance of the status quo, CLC never considered the option of *reducing* shipping rates on the west-to-east runs, thereby limiting the power of the cartel. Instead, it limited its actions to denying the scheduled increases.

Once the decision was made in connection with international shipping, the same approach was applied to the international air transport industry. Here the rates charged by American carriers on international routes were determined by agreements adopted by the Traffic Conference of the International Air Transport Association (IATA). The Cost of Living Council did not seek to control any aspect of these agreements; however, by controlling the price behavior of American carriers (the Civil Aeronautics Board acts as the approving body for the United States), restraints could be imposed on the actions of the IATA. Because there was no effort to increase air carrier rates on foreign routes during the freeze period, this ruling had no practical effect.

Equally contradictory factors entered into judgments concerning the coverage of the freeze as applied to raw agricultural products. A continuous series of decisions had to be made distinguishing between raw agricultural products, which were exempt from the freeze, and processed agricultural commodities, which were covered by the freeze. Many of these decisions were down-to-earth and enhanced the council's solomonic qualities to the amusement of the press. For example, honey remained a raw agricultural commodity even when it was "drained or strained," whereas fish and other forms of seafood were removed from this category when they were "shelled, shucked, skinned, or scaled."

The problem of definition was complicated when the agricultural product involved was subject to government price support. This circumstance was most vividly illustrated by the implications of determining when a peanut becomes a processed agricultural product. Those whose knowledge of peanuts is limited to their consumption at sporting events or distribution at zoos might reasonably believe that a peanut becomes a processed agricultural product when it is removed from the shell. This lay approach carried with it significant consequences for the federal budget. Because there was government price support for shelled peanuts, the application of a price ceiling to this commodity meant that if the ceiling was below the support price, the government would have to step in and purchase the peanuts. And in fact this situation existed in early September of 1971. Because the legislation ties the support level to parity, the government support price for peanuts had been increased during the freeze. The support price was now above the ceiling price. Consequently the federal government would be in a position where it would have to purchase up to an estimated $50 million worth of peanuts. The Department of Agriculture determined that the frugal way out of this predicament lay in defining shelled peanuts as a raw agricultural product so the price of peanuts could rise to the level of the support price as the crop came on the market. Technical documents were provided to demonstrate that a shelled peanut was in the judgment of experts a raw agricultural product analogous to wheat that had been threshed or corn that had been removed from the cob. The decisive consideration was a 1941 legal decision under the Fair Labor Standards Act whereby shelled peanuts had been ruled to be the equivalent of a raw agricultural product by the federal courts.[11] Therefore, shelled peanuts were exempt from the freeze, avoiding further strains on the federal budget.

A more sober set of decisions were made concerning the status of transfer payments and reimbursements. Some state governors, seeing the opportunity to trim expenses, asked whether increases in welfare payments were permitted during the wage-price freeze. As mentioned above with respect to low-paid Texas workers, the council ruled that welfare payments and related forms of income were transfer payments rather than wages and thus were exempt. The same reasoning was applied to alimony and other allowances.

A similar approach was taken to reimbursements under Medicare and Medicaid. These payments are made to doctors and hospitals as reimbursements which are adjusted on the basis of ex post audits. In accordance with the law, increases in Medicaid payments were to be announced during the freeze on the basis of current audits. As reimbursements, they were permitted to go into effect without challenge.

Lastly, the council ruled that dues payments to clubs, associations, and unions were to be considered a price and therefore could not be increased during the freeze. One union applied to the council to permit a previously scheduled increase in dues. Rather than giving the union the opportunity to allege that its dues were not payment for services rendered, the council resisted this irony and ruled that the union could not initiate the increase during the freeze period. The council also acted with a fine impartiality when it ordered the Girl Scouts in North Carolina to roll back a dues increase that had become effective after August 15.

Overall, the freeze was sweeping in scope. The only major exclusion was raw agricultural products, but this limitation was balanced by extending the stabilization program to state and local governments, international rate agreements, and the military establishment. It is true that the enabling statute afforded little flexibility in defining the coverage of the freeze, but it is also correct that there was little disposition for restraint at the time. Political factors and a concern for equity reinforced the basic policy decisions in such a way that for 90 days the freeze permeated most corners of the economy.

11. *Fleming* v. *Farmers Peanut Co.,* 37 F. Supp. 628 (1941); affirmed 128 F.2d 404 (1942).

V

Setting Policy: First Principles

The strategic decision to impose a wage-price freeze was made in the context of an overall plan for dealing with current economic problems. Beyond this basic determination, however, the Cost of Living Council began its task with a nearly clean slate. Because of the short time available for planning and the secretive manner in which the new economic policy had taken shape, no specific policies or detailed regulations had been drafted when the freeze was announced. Indeed, even though the freeze went into effect on the night of August 15, the executive order which gave the program its formal legal status was not signed until late on August 16. The discussion of the program at the Camp David meeting had focused primarily on the major elements of the President's economic initiatives and had given little attention to operational details.

Only two policies had been determined by statute or executive order when the freeze commenced. The first provided for the exemption of raw agricultural products. The second policy established the general formula for determining the ceilings on wages, prices, and rents. This one sliver of detailed policy, incorporated in the first section of the executive order, stated:

(a) Prices, rents, wages, and salaries shall be stabilized for a period of 90 days from the date hereof at levels not greater than the highest of those pertaining to a substantial volume of actual transactions by each individual, business, firm, or other entity of any kind during the 30-day period ending August 14, 1971, for like or similar commodities or services. If no transactions occurred in that period, the ceiling will be the highest price, rent, salary, or wage in the nearest preceding 30-day period in which transactions did occur. No person shall charge, assess, or receive directly or indirectly in any transaction prices or rents in any form higher than those permitted hereunder, and no person shall, directly or indirectly, pay or agree to pay in any transaction wages or salaries in any form, or to use any means to obtain payment of wages and salaries in any form, higher than those permitted hereunder, whether by retroactive increase or otherwise.[1]

A third policy, in effect, established a floor as well as a ceiling price or wage. That is, under the terms of the Economic Stabilization Act, price and

---

1. Executive Order 11615, *Federal Register,* Vol. 36 (August 17, 1971), p. 15727.

wage ceilings could not be less than the levels that prevailed on May 25, 1970. If the price of a commodity had declined between May 25, 1970, and the date of the imposition of the freeze, the higher price was determinate in fixing the ceiling. This provision was apparently introduced in order to protect the position of various food products whose prices had dropped since May 25, 1970.

The fact that the policy makers had little guidance other than the admonition to suppress inflation meant that they had wide latitude in formulating the principles that would govern the freeze. In the absence of specific directives, the Cost of Living Council progressively articulated a comprehensive, if not rigid, approach to policy making.

First, there was a general agreement within CLC that the freeze should be stringent and should permit only minimal movement in wages, prices, and rents. This penchant for "toughness" reflected the strategic objectives of the freeze. The purpose of the freeze was not to explore or to manipulate subtle interrelations between economic variables. It is a truism to note that the American economy is highly complex, and any effort to "manage" it during the 90-day freeze period was likely to fail. Moreover, the forward nature of many commitments and transactions created a ponderous momentum in the movement of prices and wages. Unless rigorous policies were broadly applied, significant movements in prices and wages would continue to occur. At the least, this development would perceptibly impair the credibility of the freeze. At the worst, it would reduce the freeze to a watery nullity. Consequently, the operational objective of the freeze was to have a dramatic impact on the economy by putting a lid on wage and price changes.

If the pressures under the lid were unrelieved, the appropriate reaction would be to press harder rather than finding ways to vent this pressure. This approach did not mean that the controllers would be unrelenting even if economic calamity threatened. During the course of the freeze there was an effort to monitor the impact of the rules on the supply of vital commodities. Nonetheless, the Cost of Living Council accepted the dictum that for 90 days it was more important to preserve the integrity of the freeze than to rectify marginal distortions in resource allocation.

Second, the process of policy formulation was carried forth with a zealous concern for consistency. It was recognized from the outset of the freeze that such a program would be inherently inequitable for some individuals. A freeze literally seeks to stop the processes of economic adjustment which take place over time, as when a landlord raises rents to cover the costs of increased taxes, a producer of finished products increases prices to cover increased labor costs, a company raises wages to maintain traditional relations with wages in other firms, and so on. All such decisions based on technical factors or venerable considerations of self-interest and equity would be transformed into social or even moral questions if they were dealt with during the freeze. Instead, CLC adhered to the view that during a short period of severe restraint equity could best be achieved by treating all of the economic participants uniformly. If inequities were engendered in individual cases, they represented random occurrences based on the economic unit's status on August 15 rather than any frail administrative judgment. The fact that the freeze was scheduled to last only 90 days and enjoyed public acceptance made this dialectical approach feasible. "Uniformity" and "consistency" became the general defense against allegations of unfairness and the guiding principles of policy formulation.

Third, the policy makers gave heavy weight to the need for simplicity in the nature of the rules and regulations. Aside from any inherent advantages, simplicity was an operational necessity in the overall design of the program. When the President announced the imposition of the freeze, he stated that primary reliance would be placed on voluntary compliance rather than aggressive enforcement. This approach was a technical necessity as well as a bureaucratic strength. The absence of an extensive field staff and the short duration of the freeze meant that voluntary compliance was the only realistic means. Voluntary compliance, in turn, was largely dependent upon public understanding of the rules of the game. Other things being equal, the more simple the rules, the greater the public understanding and presumably the greater the extent of voluntary compliance. In practice, this implied that the resultant policies were less likely to take account of the special circumstances that might exist in particular industries or sectors of the economy. Simplicity meant that there would be general standards applicable across the board rather than differential categories of policies that reflected special circumstances. To the extent that this approach was followed, inequities or technical distortions might result; however, this defect was transformed into a virtue since the level of generality consistent with simplicity was clearly reinforced by the desire for consistency.

Fourth, policy making during the freeze proceeded with what by normal government standards was giddy speed. Most of the major policies were determined by the Cost of Living Council in the first two weeks of the freeze. This rapid pace meant that some of the policies were formulated on the basis of inadequate staff work. On the other hand, the need for speed and comprehensive guidance to the public put a premium on general rather than specific policies. Although several missteps were made, a broad policy framework was developed in a short period of time so that rulings could be made in individual cases of considerable complexity once the initial shock of the freeze had passed.

Against this background, the character of the freeze was determined by the disposition of five key issues. These decisions dealt with technical matters such as the definition of the base period and the economic unit to which the ceiling prices applied. Together, the resultant policies constituted the linkage between the strategic objectives of the freeze, the terms of the Economic Stabilization Act, and permissible market behavior.

1. *The Definition of Wages, Prices, and Rent.* In the administration of the freeze wages, prices, and rent were defined in the broadest possible terms to insure comprehensive coverage and to minimize the extent to which the program would have a differential impact on different sectors of the economy. In this manner, the operational definition of "wages" included all forms of compensation. Because they constituted elements of labor cost, all types of fringe benefits were encompassed by the freeze. Similarly, "wages" was interpreted to mean any system of compensation rather than only the general level of wages. Therefore merit and longevity increases, job evaluation plans, profit sharing, and other incentive arrangements all fell within the scope of the freeze. The sweeping language of the pertinent OEP regulation stated:

"Wages and Salaries" includes all forms of remuneration or inducement to employees by their employers, including but not limited to: vacation and holiday payments; bonuses; layoff and supplemental unemployment insurance benefits; night shift, overtime, and other premiums; employer contributions to insurance, savings, or other welfare benefits; employer contributions to pension or annuity funds; payments in kind, job perquisites, cost-of-living allowances, expense accounts, commissions, discounts, stock options, payments for deferred compensation, and all other "fringe" benefits.

In addition, there may be no changes in working conditions which result in more pay per hour worked (for example, a schedule which shortens the work week without a proportionate decrease in pay).[2]

The definition of a "price" was equally broad, explicitly incorporating a price-quantity-quality relationship. Although subtle variations in quantity

2. OEP Stabilization Program Guideline 4.0814.

or quality would be difficult to detect or to control, this policy was formally enunciated to provide a basis for action against any violators who might be identified. In fact, the policy was invoked in a few cases where firms that had been caught with rising costs attempted to mitigate the pinch of the price freeze by withdrawing established services.

A net price was used in determining the applicable ceiling. This meant that promotions, allowances, and other discounts were included in calculating the effective ceiling price. No weight was given to published prices or to the normal pricing practices of the firm. If a firm was engaged in a promotional campaign in the base period preceding the freeze, the effective transaction price had to be used in determining the ceiling price. In some instances, particularly the wholesale groceries trade, the ceiling price was at or below cost because heavy promotional campaigns had been in effect during the 30 days prior to the freeze. Despite a concern that this approach might dry up the supply of certain goods, there is no evidence that such a shortage occurred on a widespread basis. Apparently, most wholesalers continued to provide the commodities at the promotional price in order to retain the goodwill of their customers.

Rent was treated in the same manner as prices. The rent ceiling assumed the maintenance of services and also took account of any allowances or discounts. As noted below, the definition of rents became even more restrictive when it was linked to the unit-by-unit rule which, in effect, established a separate ceiling price for each rental unit rather than categories of units in a multiple-unit residence.

2. *The Definition of a Base Period.* The definition of a base period was a critical factor in setting the limits of the actual price and wage ceilings. Generally, the shorter the base period for the calculation of the ceiling, the more likely that the ceiling would reflect extreme conditions such that the standard might be excessively high or excessively low in terms of "normal" market conditions. In the initial draft of the executive order instituting the freeze, the base period was set at one week. This period was expanded to 30 days to encompass a wider range of prices for those commodities that were characterized by significant short-term fluctuations.

The determination of the length of the base period was made by top officials at the Camp David meeting. They recognized that the duration of the base period would have a significant impact on the ceiling prices that were applicable to two major industries, steel and autos. In the case of steel, the industry had initiated a substantial price increase for many products in the two-week period between the effective date of the new labor agreement with the United Steel Workers on August 1 and the commencement of the freeze on August 15. The automobile industry, on the other hand, was scheduled to introduce new models with higher prices in the month following the imposition of the freeze.

Administration officials rejected any suggestion that the base period be adjusted to minimize the impact of the freeze on these industries. However, the automobile industry subsequently obtained a measure of relief under the terms of the seasonality rule which provided an alternative to the low ceiling that would be established by end-of-the-model-year prices that prevailed in August. The steel industry also gained some latitude as a consequence of a ruling that where a price had been raised within the base period, the determination of whether or not a substantial volume of transactions had taken place would be measured from the date on which the price had been increased. This rule was applicable to wage increases as well and reflected the Cost of Living Council's lack of authority and disposition to induce widespread rollbacks of wages or prices.

The 30-day base period definition was subject to modification in three sets of circumstances. First, under the "seasonality rule" the ceiling price for a product with demonstrated seasonal characteristics could be determined either by the price that prevailed during the 30-day base period or by the price that prevailed at the time the relevant seasonal event last occurred. To qualify under the seasonality rule, a seller had to demonstrate that the price or wage under consideration underwent a distinct fluctuation at a specific, identifiable point of time and that such fluctuations had taken place in each of the past three years.

Within the period of the freeze, the seasonality rule was most applicable to hotel and resort rates during the Labor Day weekend, wages for seasonal agricultural workers, and the ceiling price for 1972 automobiles. Under the terms of the seasonality rule, for example, automobile manufacturers and dealers could select as a ceiling price either the price that prevailed in the 30-day period prior to August 15, 1971, or the price that was charged for the equivalent models when they were introduced in the fall of 1970. This rule had economic credibility because, in fact, new automobiles generally commanded higher prices at the beginning of the sales year than at the end, and the price of hotel accommodations did rise during peak periods of demand.

As a second modification of the basic rule, when there had been an increase in published prices within the regular 30-day period, the new base was defined as the period between the time that the new price list had been published and August 15. This truncated base period applied to both wages and prices. Indeed, the treatment of wages determined the treatment of prices. For example, if wages had increased by 10 percent on August 13, this higher ceiling was maintained for the duration of the freeze. If this adjustment of the base period had not been permitted, there was a strong likelihood that wages would have to be rolled back because a "substantial volume of transactions" had not taken place at the higher rate during the normal 30-day base period. Although the same principle was extended to changes in published prices, the rule did not always provide additional room for price movements; for if goods had not actually been shipped at the higher price, then bona fide "transactions" had not taken place under the government's definition. As indicated previously, this rule afforded some relief for the steel industry, which had raised prices following the negotiation of a substantial wage increase with the steelworkers union on August 1, 1971. OEP analysts estimated that about 60 percent of the steel products on which published prices had been increased in the two weeks prior to August 15 actually qualified for a higher ceiling price. The remaining commodities had not yet been marketed and so did not figure in a "substantial volume of transactions." For these, the applicable ceiling was governed by the earlier, lower price.

The third modification of the rule applied in those cases in which particular goods had not been produced or sold during the standard 30-day period. This situation was most likely to arise in the production and sale of specialized parts or commodities sold on a sporadic basis to industrial customers. Under these circumstances, the base period was slipped back in 30-day increments until a period was reached when the good had been sold. The price that prevailed at the time constituted the ceiling price. In one extreme case, a large manufacturing firm had to calculate back two years before the date of the freeze—when the last transaction in a specialized commodity had taken place—to establish a base period.

3. *The Definition of a "Substantial Volume of Actual Transactions."* The definition of a "substantial volume of actual transactions" probably had the most decisive effect on the nature of the freeze. Within any specified base period, the actual ceiling price would be determined by defining the acceptable "transactions" for this purpose. Because transactions involving the same category of goods or services often took place at different prices and the term "transaction" was itself imprecise, the definition posed important conceptual and technical problems.

The substantiality test adopted by the Cost of Living Council was relatively liberal. It stated that 10 percent of the transactions that took place within the base period qualified as "a substantial volume."[3] This rule was adopted from past experience with controls during the Korean War and permitted the firm to use the highest prices charged during the base period for determining the legal ceiling.

It was the definition of a "transaction," however, that had the most profound impact on the permissible upward movement of wages and prices. The overriding problem in defining a transaction was how to classify those increases in prices and wages which were scheduled to take effect sometime during the freeze. At the outset of the freeze, many agreements already had been reached providing for wage hikes during the 90-day period, rent increases, or the delivery of goods at prices higher than those that had prevailed during the base period. In many instances, legal documents, such as leases and collective bargaining agreements, had been signed, and these cloaked the commitments with the "sanctity of contract." If these commitments were viewed as completed transactions, it was clear that significant increases in prices, rents, and wages would occur and severely undermine the credibility, if not the economic effectiveness, of the stabilization program. On the other hand, the fact that these agreements had been reached in good faith prior to August 15 presented a special claim for a permissive policy. Thus the definition of a "transaction" was a critical element that would determine whether the freeze would set its own glacial pace or be carried forward by the momentum of previous events.

To a large extent, the problem of dealing with future commitments had been resolved inadvertently by the Cost of Living Council. During the first week of the freeze, CLC considered the status of deferred wage increases. This issue was especially pressing because many unions and employers had negotiated contracts as much as two years before August 15, 1971, that provided for wage increases to become effective during the freeze. The Cost of Living Council decided the deferred wage increase issue independently of the related price and rent issues and determined that such increases would not be permitted during the freeze. In the following two weeks, a clamor arose from landlords and businessmen to permit scheduled rent and price increases to go into effect. Renters and buyers were equally insistent that the implementation of these scheduled increases would provide windfalls to a few and would discredit the program.

Belatedly, the council recognized that the problem of future commit-

3. Economic Stabilization Regulation 1, August 20, 1971.

ments was essentially the same for wages, prices, and rent and that a common rule should be established as a matter both of fairness and of political prudence. Ultimately, the council adopted a uniform approach to labor, commodity, and rental housing transactions by promulgating a "delivered" goods and services concept. This meant that a transaction had not taken place unless the employees actually had worked at the higher rate, the rental unit had been occupied, or the goods had been shipped by the seller. This approach effectively suspended wage and rent increases scheduled to be instituted during the freeze. Similarly, most companies could not charge the planned higher prices because they had not actually shipped 10 percent of their goods at this new price in the 30-day period prior to August 15. The ban was maintained even though bills of sale specifying the higher prices had been signed before the freeze.

4. *The Definition of the Unit for Calculating Transactions.* The definition of the unit which administrators would use in calculating transactions buttressed the restraints that had been laid down when interpreting "a substantial volume of transactions." It was important to forestall any aggregation or selection of units that would raise the wage or price ceilings above the level that otherwise would be permitted by cumulating 10 percent of the transactions within a single established unit. For instance, a national retail chain might seek to raise the price of a particular commodity to the highest level that prevailed in any individual market area before the freeze even though local pricing areas had been recognized by company executives in the past.

Although the unit for calculating transactions was never comprehensively defined, the general principle adopted was to use the most limited unit that could be identified on the basis of established practices at the time that the freeze was imposed. In this manner, the unit for calculating transactions in the product market generally was limited to the individual plant or retail outlet unless it could be demonstrated that broader units such as the firm or a regional market area were traditionally employed. Similarly, the unit of transaction for the determination of wage and salary ceilings was the contractual or administrative unit defined by past practice. This might be company-wide, plant-wide, or related to particular occupational groups.

In the case of teachers, the individual teacher was considered to be the unit of transaction because the scheduling and nature of his or her activities are usually determined by the terms of an individual contract. In addition, the use of this extremely narrow unit of transaction blocked efforts to win higher wages for all teachers in a particular school district on the grounds that a few had started to work at higher salary levels there in the weeks immediately preceding the imposition of the freeze. As indicated elsewhere, the consequences of this ruling were extremely controversial and precipitated complicated legal proceedings in various state and federal courts. Nevertheless, the technical definition of the unit of transaction in this case was consistent with the political judgment that so large and visible a group as teachers should not be insulated from the freeze because of the unique nature and timing of the employment relationship.

A special unit-by-unit rule was applied to rental housing. Under this provision, each apartment was considered a unit in its own right for purposes of defining the appropriate base period and ceiling price. This interpretation was highly restrictive and meant, for example, that if a landlord had raised the rental on nine out of ten apartments in an apartment complex before the freeze, this would not provide a legal basis for increasing the rent in the remaining, tenth apartment. In effect, the actual rent that was paid on the apartment in the base period preceding the freeze became the applicable price during the freeze.

This stringent approach to the determination of rental transaction units reflected several considerations. First, there was an appreciation of the keen political sensitivity to increases in rent. Although rent constituted only 5 percent of the consumer price index, this charge was a substantial proportion of the monthly expenditures of those who did not own their own residences. Second, the unit-by-unit rule had been applied during World War II. Third, the formal justification for this principle was the contention that each rental unit was distinctive and therefore constituted a separate "product." The unit-by-unit rule was subjected to legal challenge in the courts but was upheld in several cases.[4]

5. *The Definition of Allowable Pass-Through of Cost Increases.* The freeze had its most forceful effect on those enterprises which incurred rising costs before price adjustments could be made and in cases in which the price of uncontrolled items such as raw agricultural products had risen after August 15. The obvious effect of these increases in costs was to narrow profit margins. Anguished petitions for relief were soon forthcoming

---

4. The leading case was *United States* v. *Lieb,* 333 F. Supp. 424 (W.D. Tex. 1971). The status of the unit-by-unit rule was affirmed by the Temporary Emergency Court of Appeals, 462 F.2d 1161 (1972), TECA having been established to handle cases arising under the stabilization program. The Lieb case involved a suit initiated during the freeze.

from many businessmen, particularly those who processed agricultural products or who fabricated basic steel products. In the latter case, the prices charged for many product lines had been raised shortly before the freeze.

Again, the disposition of the policy makers toward "toughness" and uniformity of treatment determined the policy concerning the issue. Because of the relatively short duration of the freeze and the overriding objective of putting the brakes on price increases, a general policy was adopted denying any application for a cost pass-through. Requests for the lifting of a price ceiling because of cost increases would be considered only on the basis of "gross inequities" as provided by the Economic Stabilization Act.[5] In practice, no private firm ever met the test of a gross inequity even though bankruptcy threatened as a consequence of the increase in costs.

Some relief from the pressure of increased costs was afforded in certain categorical circumstances reflecting governmental actions or well-established pricing and wage practices. Firms could pass on the increased price of an imported good that was sold in its original form if such an increase was attributable to the imposition of the import surcharge. However, the surcharge could be passed through only on a penny-for-penny basis and could not be incorporated in the base for the calculation of percentage markups. Also, if the imported product was transformed in any way or became a component of another product, the increased cost could not be passed through. Rents could be increased in accordance with a fixed formula if convincing evidence was presented that a significant investment had been made in capital improvements before or during the freeze.[6] Insurance rates could rise on the basis of predetermined formulae linking rate changes to actuarial experience, but the higher rates could not be justified by increases in administrative costs. In the wage area, some analogous pass-throughs were blessed by permitting wage increases if there was

5. P.L. 91-379 (August 15, 1970), sec. 202. The administrative definition of a "gross inequity" is discussed in Chap. VI.

6. The following criteria were applied to rent increases for improvements: "(1) The capital improvement must equal at least three months' rent (with a minimum of $250) on items that would be classified as capital improvements by the Internal Revenue Service. (2) If condition (1) is met, the unit may be treated as a new apartment, with rent to be no higher than the rent charged on comparable apartments in the market area, subject to the limitation that the monthly rent may not increase by more than 1½ percent of the amount spent for capital improvement." OEP Stabilization Program Guideline 3.1716.

a bona fide promotion, if an employee had completed prescribed educational requirements or an apprentice program, or if increased contributions for fringe benefit programs were paid to cover higher costs without a change in the benefit levels.

Overall, the basic policies governing the freeze imposed formidable restraints on upward price and wage movements during the freeze. The concept of a transaction and the determination of the base period sharply minimized the discretion of most businesses in their wage and price decisions. The general prohibition of cost pass-through meant that no weight would be given to changing economic conditions. The exceptions made to these rules provided for only limited adjustments, and they had to be based on demonstrable historical practices. Other special circumstances, such as an increase in costs because of higher taxes, because of safety or ecological standards imposed by the government, or because of rising prices for raw materials, were all explicitly disallowed as a basis for exception. For 90 days the economy would function within the narrow boundaries defined by these fundamental policies.

VI

Setting Policy: Second Principles

The policies formulated by the Cost of Living Council were not self-effectuating. Rather, they established general guides to administration in particular cases. It is axiomatic that the American economy encompasses a complexity of special circumstances that cannot be accommodated by broad statements of policy. As the 90-day period progressed, the problems of interpretation and administration became increasingly varied, if not arcane, and complex reasoning often became necessary to preserve the overall integrity of the basic policies. Whereas in the first month of the freeze the Cost of Living Council had to determine the extent to which seasonal factors would modify the basic policy governing the definition of the base period, by the middle of October the CLC staff was giving sober consideration to whether or not Halloween candy adorned with a special wrapper met the requirements of the seasonality rule. And once a policy was adopted permitting the limited pass-through of an import surcharge, the council had to decide whether the added dollar volume of sales permitted by this pass-through could be used in calculating salesmen's commissions or rental charges for retail stores which were based on sales volume.

As an administrative reality, it was impossible to formulate and apply policies only at the general level; inevitably, the momentum of controls and the cumulative occurrence of special situations forced the policy makers and staff to give attention to the trees in order to preserve the forest. It is true, of course, that the fate of the Republic or even the outcome of the battle against inflation did not hinge upon whether or not Halloween candy qualified under the seasonality rule or whether cucumbers are a raw or processed agricultural product. But for those who produced and sold Halloween candy or cucumbers, these decisions had a profound financial effect and warranted serious attention. Unlike other macro-economic policies, controls must give consideration to specific cases and the due process that this implies.

Definition and Identification

The first set of administrative problems involved questions of definition and identification. Although the operational concept of a "wage" or a "price" was broadly conceived from the outset, specific cases soon proliferated that were not obviously covered by the existing definitions. When one university was blocked from giving a scheduled salary increase, it offered to provide faculty members with interest-free loans instead. These interest-free loans were subsequently ruled to be wages and therefore could not be extended under the terms of the freeze.

Equally exotic cases arose on the price side. One firm was proscribed from raising the deposit or down payment on the purchase of a commodity on the grounds that this action constituted an increase in price. More controversial was a determination that municipal charges for water and sewerage services were a "price" and therefore could not be increased during the freeze. Local practices in defraying the costs of such services varied widely. In some municipalities, the costs were paid from general tax funds; in other cases, individual charges were made for services on the basis of use.

The Cost of Living Council adopted a literal approach to determining whether or not a price was involved. Where a fee for the service was charged, this was considered to be a price and could not be increased. On the other hand, if the services were financed through taxes, taxes could be raised to cover increased costs or to generate additional revenues. Although some philosophical argument could be made that taxes constituted a form of a price, a "price" was presumed to exist for purposes of the stabilization program only in relation to the specific purchase of a good or a service and only where the incidence of the charge was to an individual or corporate user. This distinction was not easily perceived by the public, and throughout the freeze the Cost of Living Council received a steady stream of complaints calling for the application of the freeze to taxes.

In a similar case, the state of Pennsylvania had passed a law requiring all persons who purchased liquor to have an identification card. A flat dollar charge was to be paid for the identification card. A complaint was lodged alleging that the institution of a charge for the identification card constituted the imposition of a price where no charge had been made in the past. The Cost of Living Council staff backed out of this corner by classifying the identification card as a "license" designed to regulate the consumption of alcoholic beverages by particular classes of the population rather than a "price" for a service. Thus taxes and license fees were outside the scope of regulation, while fees charged for specific services were subject to limitation.

Ambiguities had to be resolved in the rental area also. For example, owners of cooperative or condominium apartments usually pay monthly charges to cover costs associated with the general maintenance of the building. In many instances, these monthly charges were scheduled to increase during the 90-day period. If these charges were viewed as comparable to rent, the increases clearly could be prohibited by the terms of the freeze. However, the particular form of ownership in a cooperative or condominium meant that these maintenance charges were, in effect, operating costs incurred by the individual owners. Consequently, they were exempted from the freeze. More subtly, when the condominium was managed by an agent, the agent's charges levied on the owners of individual apartments were frozen, whereas the charges incurred for maintenance services could be increased. In strictly economic terms, the distinction between maintenance services and management services is difficult to defend, if not to fathom. Nonetheless, this distinction bowed to the legal niceties of the situation while assuaging condominium owners who inevitably believed that they should receive the best of both worlds.

The difference in the rules applicable to prices and rents lent considerable significance to rulings on whether a charge was identified as a price or a rental fee. As noted above, prices were subject to the 10 percent rule in determining a substantial volume of transactions, while the rent ceilings were established on a unit-by-unit basis. Both analytically and administratively, the problem of deciding which rule applied was particularly troublesome if lodging was intertwined with other services. This issue arose in two important categories of cases: charges for hospital rooms and charges for room and board as part of college tuition.

Analytically, some part of the total charge for a hospital room goes for the room itself, and another part is related to the medical services and overhead associated with the room. It was technically possible to segregate the housing costs from the medical costs and to apply the rental rules to the former and the rule governing prices to the latter. Any penchant for purism was quickly overwhelmed, however, by the predictable administrative difficulties. In addition, estimates of the distribution of costs clearly indicated that a preponderant proportion of the charge for a hospital room was for medical services rather than lodging. Accordingly, hospital room charges were classified as a price and therefore were covered by the applicable rules.

The problem of dealing with college room and board charges was complicated by the Cost of Living Council's earlier ruling on college tuition. It will be recalled that colleges generally were permitted to raise tuition even though the educational services had not been delivered. Here the reasoning was that through the conveyance of a deposit a transaction had been completed before the new school year commenced. The Cost of Living Council glumly recognized that it was bound by a policy that was awkward at best and inconsistent with the general transaction rule. This unease was accentuated when trying to distinguish between room and board fees in dormitories operated by the educational institution and the rents charged for student housing units operated by agents or private owners. Under the rules applicable to residences in general, the rents could not be raised if a unit had not been occupied at the higher rate. However, if dormitory fees were treated like tuition charges, the payment of a deposit would have been sufficient to consummate a "transaction," thereby permitting the higher rate to become effective. After considerable bureaucratic writhing, the CLC staff attempted to straddle the issue. If the dormitory or housing facility was operated by the college or university and if a deposit had been provided by the student before the freeze, then the higher charge could go into effect. If the housing unit was owned or operated by a private party, then the unit-by-unit rule governing other rental properties was applicable. Intellectually, this distinction made little sense; but it did serve to preserve a narrow consistency with the initial ruling concerning tuition and preserved any goodwill that had been created with college administrators through the earlier determination.

An analogous problem arose in determining the status of "points" charged for obtaining a mortgage. Under this widespread practice a flat charge, based on a percentage of the mortgage, was levied on the borrower. Numerous complaints were received that lending institutions had raised the percentage rate for these charges. If the points were viewed as a price, they were frozen at pre-existing levels; if they were considered to be a component of the actual interest on the loan, they were exempted. In this case, the council staff followed obvious economic logic and classified such points as interest outside the scope of controls.

In addition to the extremely detailed problems of trying to disentangle joint products or services, the Cost of Living Council had to make almost metaphysical judgments concerning certain phenomena that were easily understood in principle but extremely abstruse in application. For example, council regulations specified that when a "new product" was offered for sale the ceiling would be determined by the price "realized on the same or comparable product or service by the most nearly comparable competitor."[1] A parallel concept was used in dealing with new apartments and family housing units.

Though this principle was simple in concept, its administrative feasibility was determined by the definition of a "new product." After a wide search of the literature and consultation with industry representatives, the CLC staff affirmed that "a product or service is new if it is substantially different from other products or services in purpose, function, or technology or if its use results in a substantially different outcome."[2] Obviously, so abstract a definition would have to be refined as it was applied to specific cases. Nonetheless, the council was anxious to promulgate some standard in order to prevent systematic evasion of the price ceilings by allegations that a particular product was new or significantly different from established products. Because of the short duration of the freeze, few cases of this nature arose, and the ambiguity in the definition was not rigorously tested or revealed.

Even where definitional problems were minimal, the process of administration frequently was complicated by questions of identification and data collection. In this respect, at an early stage of the program, the Cost of Living Council ruled that futures contracts in commodities markets should be subject to the freeze. Even though this decision could hardly be justified in economic terms, the step was taken to defend the administration against charges that "speculators" were free to reap profits during the freeze. Following this decision, CLC ruled that the ceiling price for futures contracts would be determined by the spot prices that were in effect at the individual exchanges for the particular commodity during the 30-day base period prior to August 15, 1971. Once this net was cast, the problem of implementation was formidable. First, it had to be determined whether there would be separate prices for individual traders or for the exchange in general. Second, responsibility for computing the ceiling price had to be assigned. Third, if no spot prices were available for the base period in the particular commodity at the individual exchange, what futures prices would be applicable?

---

1. OEP Economic Stabilization Circular 102 (October 20, 1971), sec. 402(2).
2. *Ibid.*, sec. 401(1).

Ultimately, operational answers were given to all of these questions. The ruling was passed down that the ceiling price should be calculated on an exchange-wide basis by the exchange itself, and if base period spot prices were not available, the futures price that prevailed on the date nearest the beginning of the base period should be used to determine the ceiling. But as the program progressed, it was clear that the problems of obtaining, classifying, and organizing the data were so great that no one was quite sure what the actual ceiling price should be in an individual case. Like the emperor's clothes, a fabric of regulations was spun out no matter how vaporous the cloth might be.

Problems of Implementation

The difficulties of identifying the ceiling price for futures contracts was indicative of a broader problem of administration. The comprehensive coverage of the freeze dictated that the policies be equally comprehensive in scope. But in many instances it soon became obvious that effective control was a practical impossibility because of the nature of the commodities under consideration or technical problems of enforcement beyond the capabilities of the existing staff. Thus commodities sold at auction or subject to competitive bids were formally included in the freeze. Explicit rules covering these cases were duly promulgated for the guidance of the public. However, the tenuous nature of this action was illustrated by the rule stating that the ceiling price of a work of art was the price for the most "comparable work" sold in the base period. Nonetheless, the Cost of Living Council sought to maintain the public fiction that such commodities were subject to regulation. The general strategy was to create sufficient restraint, if not uncertainty, so that the sellers would have a bias in favor of the status quo and lower prices rather than higher prices. It was almost an act of whimsy when, in response to an impassioned plea from the American Philatelic Society, the council solemnly stated that the price of used stamps bought and sold by collectors was subject to the price freeze and could not be increased. Obviously, no effective measures could be taken to enforce this stricture.

In some instances, this combination of rigorous policy formulation and administrative evasion could not be sustained, and specific decisions had to be made to resolve problems posed by the initial policy judgment. For example, although the communications and entertainment media had been exempted from previous ventures in price control, they were covered by the 1971 stabilization effort. In particular, the freeze was imposed shortly before the onset of the new television season when the networks were in the process of determining the applicable advertising rates. To implement the freeze, a judgment had to be made whether the ceiling for advertising rates was related to specific time periods or to individual programs as priced in the fall of 1970. In practice, advertising rates reflected the expected audience size, which depended on both the time slot and the attractiveness of the specific program. Because the popularity of a new program was uncertain, the rate charged for it would ordinarily be influenced by the time slot. On the other hand, a program with demonstrated drawing power might command high rates in various time periods.

The formula adopted by the Cost of Living Council allowed the networks a measure of discretion to take account of the fact that the complementary effects of a particular program and a particular time slot on the expected audience could not be precisely determined. The network was given an option in choosing the ceiling for advertising rates; if the program had played previously, the ceiling could be either the rate charged for the same program during the base period or the rate charged for the same time slot during the base period, which could be modified by the seasonality rule when applicable. Each network or station had to use either the "program" or "time slot" approach consistently in setting the rate schedule for established programs. For new programs, the ceiling on advertising rates was set by the rate charged for the time slot last season.

Perhaps the most consequential problem of implementation involved the seasonality rule. The application of this policy presented no administrative difficulties in well-defined, traditional cases such as Labor Day rates for hotels and the introduction of new automobile models. In other situations, however, eligibility for the seasonality rule was not clear. The status of apparel was particularly ambiguous. Again, the timing of the freeze had a direct impact on the prices that could be charged for new fall and winter apparel coming on the market in August and September. New fashions could qualify for the seasonality rule, but practice in the industry was sufficiently varied so that a blanket ruling could not be made. Moreover, with the introduction of the fall and winter styles taking place continuously throughout the freeze, it was not possible to handle the problem in a once-and-for-all manner. Consequently, except for dealing with a few flagrant cases, only limited efforts were made to refine and apply the seasonality rule rigorously to the apparel trade. Both the incidence of consumer complaints and movements in the apparel component of the consumer price index indicated that the inability to sharpen the application of the seasonality rule resulted in price increases that probably exceeded the amounts that would have been permissible under a strict interpretation of the policy.

The variety and complexity of collective bargaining practices also necessitated dexterity in the implementation of the general policies concerning negotiated wage increases. Under the transactions rule, a wage increase was permissible under a collective bargaining agreement if the agreement had been reached prior to August 15. As a practical matter, the collective bargaining process did not always lend itself to a definitive judgment of when an agreement was actually "reached" for purposes of the stabilization program. In the telephone industry, for example, an agreement was reached between the Communications Workers of America and major components of the Bell Telephone System on Monday, July 13. The agreement could not be formally ratified until a referendum vote of the union's members had been taken. The results of the referendum were not announced until after the freeze had been in effect. In another case, the Screen Actors Guild had negotiated an agreement with the motion picture firms in July 1971. However, the agreement was not formally approved by August 15 because a mail poll of the members, who were dispersed throughout the world, was necessary.

In each situation, a formal determination had to be made whether, in fact and in law, the agreement had been "reached" and was in effect prior to August 15. The Cost of Living Council used a rule of reason such that if a new contract had been agreed to by negotiation but had not been technically ratified, it was considered to have been reached. Following this approach, the wage increases negotiated by the Communications Workers and the Guild were approved.

Problems of Adjustment and Equity

In addition to problems of technical interpretation, the process of policy implementation was conditioned by questions of adjustment and equity. Although the theory of the freeze posited an unremitting approach to possible price or wage increases, this position was impossible to sustain on a comprehensive basis. Even the most inflexible administrator was forced to concede the need for adjustments because of past economic events or overwhelming inequities. At the same time, there was little disposition to approve those changes in business practices which could be construed as efforts to circumvent the general policies governing the stabilization program.

The limits of the freeze were tested in determining the extent to which prices, wages, and rents could increase in accordance with established formulae. In the insurance industry, rates normally were adjusted on the basis of actuarial experience. Many employees were covered by compensation plans whereby earnings fluctuated with output, sales, or profits. And in some public housing units, rents could be increased in accordance with changes in the tenant's income.

As an extreme application of the freeze, any wage or price increases under the operation of these formulae could have been proscribed. This alternative was rejected on the grounds that the price or wage was fixed by the formulae and that as long as the formulae were unchanged the freeze had not been violated. The decisive consideration was the knowledge that a flat ban on formula-related increases would effectively render inoperative incentive plans which tied compensation to output. Accordingly, insurance premiums could be increased on the basis of actuarial experience, but no upward adjustments could be made because of increases in administrative costs. Similarly, earnings were permitted to rise under the normal operation of incentive, commission, and profit-sharing plans as long as the formulae and the base wage rates were not modified. In one unusual case, gold miners in Idaho were entitled to a bi-weekly bonus based on fluctuations in the price of gold. This practice was permitted to continue.

A different approach was taken where increases were linked to the completion of service requirements, probationary periods, or apprenticeship training programs. In some situations workers receive substantial wage increases upon completion of certain stages of apprenticeship or following a probationary period of employment. Many employers also provide for "step increases" based on longevity of service. The latter practice is especially prevalent among teachers and government employees in general. As a general matter, the Cost of Living Council rejected the notion that the passage of time alone or the completion of service constituted an acceptable basis for wage increases. This position had been taken in dealing with deferred wage increases scheduled to take effect during the freeze, and the principle was extended to cases involving individuals. A distinction was made, however, between wage increases related to simple service requirements and those linked to completion of an apprentice program or the earning of an advanced college degree, as was the case in many educational systems. Here, completion of the program or attainment of the degree was viewed as a proxy for a promotion or an increase in productivity, and the wage raise was permitted.

Probationary increases fell between the two principles. On the one hand, wage increases were given after the completion of a prescribed period of time and were not directly related to the completion of any formal training program. On the other hand, it was recognized that a probationary period served as the occasion for intensive on-the-job training and evaluation of the new employee by the employer. These two considerations were arbitrarily balanced by allowing probationary increases when the probationary period did not exceed three months. If the period exceeded three months, the increases were viewed as analogous to longevity increments; up to that time, greater weight was given to the training and evaluation aspects. Whether or not these rulings were defensible on a theoretical level, they did provide a practical basis for permitting some adjustments that otherwise would have been foreclosed by the general policies of the freeze.

The effort to preserve a logical and uniform structure of rules also faltered when the implications of these rules were manifestly onerous or inequitable. As noted previously, the council had stated that scheduled raises in wages or benefits could not take place during the freeze. This economic blackout had a heavy impact on individuals whose status during the freeze would determine the flow of benefits at the conclusion of the freeze. Pension benefits for an employee are frequently fixed by the level of earnings of the employee at the time of his retirement. In the normal course of events, many workers reached retirement during the 90-day period. If a wage increase scheduled for sometime between August 15 and the retirement date of the employee was blocked by the freeze, the wage base for the calculation of the employee's pension would be reduced accordingly. The economic impact of this action on the individual worker would, of course, far transcend the freeze. In addition to this egregious situation, some benefits, such as medical insurance, could be elected only once a year. If an employee was denied the right to exercise this option, another twelve months would have to pass before the opportunity was available again.

When these circumstances came to light through inquiries and complaints, the existing rules were hastily modified, and cases decided under the old rules could be reopened. Employees could accrue increases in benefits during the freeze where election was limited to particular dates. Similarly, the higher wage rate could be used as the basis for calculating an employee's pension even though this rate did not become effective until the freeze had ended.

The effort to maintain consistency precipitated an even greater outcry from the affected parties when the general policies were applied to the operation of vacation plans. Using the "time is not enough" criterion, CLC ruled that employees who became eligible for additional weeks of paid vacation because they met specified length-of-service requirements during the freeze could not exercise this right because it represented an increase in compensation. The purity of the principle involved was incomprehensible to the normal worker; and those who presumed to understand it found it to be grossly inequitable. After the council staff was assailed by a barrage of complaints and several rounds of reconsideration, this rule was relaxed to permit eligible employees to take the additional vacation time.

The pressures to modify or relax the general policies were most acute where collective bargaining was involved. The effect of collective bargaining was to accentuate equity considerations while formalizing practices that otherwise would be hard to validate. One of the more contentious issues dealt with by the Cost of Living Council had to do with the status of retroactive wage increases. When a labor contract expires in collective bargaining, the employees often will continue to work as the result of an agreement that any wage increase subsequently negotiated will be retroactive to the expiration date of the contract. Similarly, there may be an agreement to pay retroactively even if negotiations break down at some point and a strike takes place.

When the freeze was imposed on August 15, these circumstances existed in several cases. That is, the bargaining agreement had expired prior to the freeze. A new agreement reached during the freeze provided for retroactive pay at the increased wage rates back to the date of the contract expiration. Under normal practice these higher rates would, of course, be paid, but the cases referred to fell within the time boundaries of the freeze, and this practice ran afoul of the council's policies because under existing rules transactions had not taken place at the higher wages in the base period. Moreover, some council members feared that permitting retroactive increases to continue throughout the freeze period would open the door for systematic evasion. These arguments were countered by the contention that retroactivity was a highly constructive practice in American industrial relations and contributed significantly to the maintenance of industrial peace.

The issue came to the full Cost of Living Council as a narrow question of whether or not a higher wage that was retroactive to a date prior to

August 15 would be permitted to continue in effect during the freeze. The council formally considered the question on four different occasions, and the solution decided upon was awkward at best. The council specified that wage increases could be applied retroactively for the time before August 15 (but not for the time after August 15) if it was demonstrated in specific instances that retroactivity was a past practice and had not been agreed to in order to offset the effect of the freeze. Thereafter, through the duration of the freeze, the wage rate in question would be reduced to the level that was in effect before the retroactive increase was added. Ironically, this proposal was actively supported by the Secretary of Labor and opposed by other members of the council even though the consequences of the decision were nonsensical or disruptive in the context of American industrial relations.

The equivocal position of the Cost of Living Council toward established bargaining arrangements contrasted noticeably with the firm reaction to changes in business practices which might result in price increases. Whether these changes were attempted in innocence or as an adaptation to the limits imposed by the freeze, the council's response was to restrict the firm to past practice or to direct compensating adjustments if the change resulted in price increases. For example, complaints were received during the freeze that some retail outlets had discontinued the use of trading stamps. The trading stamps were determined to be "things of value," and their discontinuance raised the net price to the customer. The council ruled that retail outlets could discontinue trading stamps if the value of the stamps was passed on to the customers in the form of lower prices in either of two ways. They could reduce the prices of all goods sold by the value of the stamps, or they could deduct the value of the stamps at the cash register from the prices of those items for which trading stamps would have been given. The value of the stamps was assessed at the market value at which they could be redeemed and not at the cost to the retailer.

Other firms attempted more complex changes in pricing methods to compensate for restrictions dictated by the freeze. In the meat packing industry some firms purchase carcasses and break them into various cuts for sale to retailers or the final customer. Normally, the particular cuts are priced individually. Because shifts in demand for the different cuts occur, the price ratios between the cuts are altered periodically in order to maximize the sales value of each carcass. When the freeze was imposed in the summer, the demand for steak—and the resultant price—was at a seasonal peak. Other cuts, such as roasts, were relatively lower priced because of similar seasonal factors. After Labor Day the demand for steaks usually decreases, and prices soften; while the demand for roasts increases, and prices move upward. As the freeze progressed, these shifts in demand started to take place, but the price ratio between steak and roasts could not be changed because of the ceiling price that had been established for roasts during the base period when the demand for this cut was slack. Consequently the sales value per carcass was reduced.

Some processing firms reacted to this constraint by seeking to expand the pricing unit from individual cuts to a whole carcass. In this manner, the firm could use the decline in the price of steaks as an offset for an increase in the price of roasts, thereby maintaining the total revenue derived from the carcass. This modification of pricing methods was prohibited by the council. Those firms that sold beef by the individual cut during the base period could not shift to sales by the carcass during the freeze. Those firms that had priced and sold on a carcass basis during the base period could continue this practice.

Similar efforts were made to aggregate the unit of transaction in order to provide wide discretion in determining the ceiling price. The American Telephone and Telegraph Company (AT & T) bases advertising rates for the Yellow Pages on the number of telephones in a designated geographical area. The resultant rate schedule is highly detailed, nationwide in application, and revised continuously. However, each company in the system administers the rate schedule in its area and arranges publication of the Yellow Pages on its own initiative. As the freeze commenced, a new, higher rate schedule had been introduced by some of the individual companies in the system. AT & T explored the possibility of applying the new rate schedule throughout the system on the grounds that it had been introduced by particular companies. The council staff replied that, since the established unit for determining a substantial volume of transactions was the individual company rather than the system as a whole, the higher rates could not be extended to the units of the system that had not yet modified their schedules.

The most severe economic pressure was exerted on those firms that were caught between an increase in the price of raw materials, on the one hand, and the policy prohibiting the pass-through of costs, on the other. Where the margin between cost and price was narrow, profits were squeezed, and some companies might be forced to maintain a price that was below cost. This economic pincer was felt in many sectors of the steel fabricating industry. As noted previously, the large steel companies had raised the price of basic steel immediately before the freeze in response to the substantial wage increase that had been negotiated with the United Steelworkers of America. In almost all cases, the steel fabricators had not had time to reflect this increased cost in their prices before August 15. The prohibition of cost pass-throughs meant that the additional cost of the basic steel components would have to be absorbed by the fabricator.

Some of the fabricators sought to extricate themselves from this predicament by shifting the incidence of the cost to their customers. Normally, the fabricator bought the steel from the basic steel producers and quoted a price to the customer that included the cost of the raw material and the fabrication operation. After the price of steel was increased, some fabricators informed their customers that they would charge only for the fabrication but that the customer would have to purchase the steel and supply it to the fabricator. The consequence of this proposed arrangement would be to shift the higher cost of the steel to the final customer. The customers reacted to the obvious arithmetic of this change and filed a complaint with OEP. After consultation with the council staff, OEP informed the fabricators that they could elect to stop selling any product, but if they continued to sell, they had to provide the fabricated steel under the same arrangements as in the base period. Most of the fabricators apparently chose to absorb the cost while abiding by OEP's ruling.

Conflict with Other Government Policies

The most recurrent problem in the conduct of the freeze was the conflict between the stabilization policies and other public policies, such as the minimum wage and agricultural price support programs, that increased wages or other costs and thus exerted upward pressure on prices. As a legal matter, the Justice Department indicated that the Cost of Living Council had the authority to modify the application of these policies. But this alternative was infeasible in many cases and in other situations would probably entail greater political costs than the administration could be expected to bear. Within the framework of severe restraint, the general reaction of CLC was a mixture of principle and pragmatism.

Both the federal government and most states have adopted minimum wage laws. No extensions in coverage or increases in the minimum were scheduled under the federal statute. In Maine and Connecticut, however, the state minimum wage was scheduled to be raised during the 90-day period. The council permitted these increases to take effect because they reflected a general social judgment concerning minimum income standards for the labor force.

A different approach was taken to statutes governing the minima for workers in specific industries or occupations. As a result of the controversy ensuing from President Nixon's suspension of the Davis-Bacon Act, mentioned in Chapter I, the major construction unions had agreed to participate in the Construction Industry Stabilization Committee (CISC), the tripartite body set up under the authority of the Economic Stabilization Act. With the formation of CISC, Davis-Bacon was reinstituted. Hence the applicability of the Davis-Bacon Act was a highly sensitive issue in both economic and political terms.

CLC reacted to this situation by adopting a position which gave effect to the operation of Davis-Bacon while preserving some semblance of wage discipline. Wage increases resulting from the application of the prevailing rate concept were allowed during the freeze. The technical justification for this decision was that the wage rate applied to a particular occupation and the prevailing rate survey conducted by the Department of Labor was merely a lagged method of certifying the existence of a rate that was already in existence. But in making the determinations the Department of Labor could use only those wage rates in effect in the base period prior to August 15. Presumably, this prevented the use of Davis-Bacon as a lever to further increase construction wages during the freeze. In fact, the Secretary of Labor and Cost of Living Council were placing the greatest reliance on the effectiveness of CISC to limit construction wage increases.

A less tolerant policy was adopted toward increases in state-prescribed minima for specific occupations. In several states, the legislature establishes a minimum salary level for certain occupational groups, especially teachers. Shortly before the freeze, a few states had enacted laws raising the minima for all school districts. The salary increases required by the higher minima were blocked by CLC. The distinctions between the position taken on Davis-Bacon and the state occupational minima were somewhat strained but did have credibility. First, CLC already had ruled that increases for state and local government employees could not take effect even when they were authorized by legislative bodies. Second, the Davis-Bacon Act used a prevailing rate concept which extended existing wage levels. Raising the entire salary structure for an occupation could not be construed as maintaining an existing level. It was recognized that in many cases employee organizations sought to interpret minimum-pay laws so as to gain a general wage increase.

On a related matter, the council did permit adjustments in wages where the increases were necessary to remedy illegal practices. For example, both the federal government and various states have equal pay laws banning wage discrimination based on sex or race. If it were found that an employer had paid a lower, discriminatory wage to women in the same job classification as men, the wages of women could be raised without violating the freeze.

In contrast to the rule of reason applied to statutory wage increases, little flexibility was shown when compulsory changes in production methods resulted in higher costs for the businessman. Cost increases arising from government regulations were treated as being no different than any other cost increases. The basic policy denying the pass-through of costs was considered to be so critical to the success of the stabilization program that adjustments were allowed only in unique or severe circumstances that could be distinguished clearly from other petitions for relief. Many employers had incurred additional costs because of the requirements of the Occupational Safety and Health Act of 1970 and various anti-pollution statutes. Under CLC rules, price increases to cover the additional costs were denied. For example, when a public utility contended that it had to use more expensive, higher-quality coal to meet the standards of a state anti-pollution law, this circumstance was not considered a sufficient justification for superseding the general prohibition of cost pass-throughs. The request was rejected.

The freeze also conflicted with public financing requirements. The city of Los Angeles had floated a bond issue to finance an improvement in the municipality's sewerage system. The prospectus for the bond issue stated that use rates would be increased to finance the improvement, and buyers had purchased the bonds on this expectation. The increase in rates was scheduled to take effect after August 15 and was blocked by an OEP ruling, later sustained by the council. It was recognized that this action might pose a major problem to the city and, indeed, could precipitate a lawsuit by the bondholders. Nonetheless, a hardline position was adopted in the expectation that rates could be raised on November 14.

Perhaps the most vexing problem of balancing the stabilization program with the objectives of other government programs involved agricultural price supports and related subsidies. Under some support programs, prices could be increased on the basis of predetermined formulae. In other instances, the combined effect of the freeze and a support program was to compress profit margins or to create windfalls for individual producers. While the Cost of Living Council initially responded to these problems with puritanical zeal, it was forced to make a series of compromises for practical and political reasons.

The first case to confront the council involved price supports for peanuts. The support price for this commodity had been raised two days before the freeze in accordance with legislation which linked the support price to parity. The market price for peanuts then rose accordingly. Because of the ceiling imposed by the base period transactions rule major processors of peanuts, such as peanut butter manufacturers, could not respond to the price increase by raising the price of their own products. Many processors reacted to this pressure on margins by curtailing their purchases of peanuts. As peanut stocks accumulated, the government had to come into the market and buy at the new support price. The council refused to relax its rules, and the result of this exercise was to increase government expenditures. Although the amount of the extra expenditures cannot be measured precisely, it is estimated that government purchases of peanuts were about $20 million higher than they would have been in the absence of the freeze.

Similar circumstances arose in connection with the federal milk marketing program. Here a modicum of relief was provided by supplementary government action. Under the terms of the program, the minimum price for approximately 60 percent of all raw milk is determined by federal milk marketing orders issued for various regions. The price set by an order is in turn fixed by a formula that reflects changes in the price of manufacturing grade milk in Minnesota and Wisconsin. Utilizing this formula, the U.S. Department of Agriculture (USDA) published during the freeze an order providing for a 6 cents per hundredweight increase in the price of raw milk in one of the marketing regions. As a raw agricultural product unprocessed milk was exempted from the freeze. This price increase directly raised the costs of milk to dairy-product processors and manufacturers by an equivalent amount. However, processed milk products such as butter and cheese were covered by the stabilization program, and so the manufacturers could not translate this cost increase into higher prices for their products. Representatives of the milk processors argued strenuously to persuade the council to permit a pass-through of costs. The council denied this request, but the Department of Agriculture provided some relief by reducing the disposal price of its butter stocks to 4 cents below the normal level, putting downward pressure on prices paid by processors for milk.

The distribution of the costs of the freeze was also an important consideration in the sugar processing industry. Normally, sugar growers sell cane to sugar mills that produce raw sugar for sale to refiners. In some cases, there is vertical integration extending from the growers to the millers and the refiners. The process of production takes place within the framework of a complicated system of controls, price supports, and quotas created by the terms of the Sugar Act of 1948. Each month, the Agricultural Stabilization and Conservation Service of the USDA sets a target price for raw sugar that is determined by increases in the wholesale price index and farmers' costs. A projection is then made of the expected total demand for sugar in the United States and the proportion of this demand that could be satisfied through domestic production. The remainder is distributed by quota to foreign producers who can sell sugar in this country at the specified target price.

As the freeze commenced, the phasing of operations at the various stages of the production process had created a differential price situation which, in effect, provided the refiners with windfall profits. The mills that turn cane into raw sugar normally operate only a short period during the year when the domestic sugar crop is harvested. In contrast, refiners operate throughout the year, purchasing "raws" through imports when domestic supplies are no longer available. A new target price had been set for raw sugar prior to August 15, but the higher price had been paid only for imported sugar in the 30-day base period. The ceiling price applicable to the raw sugar produced by the sugar millers using domestic sugar cane was limited to the price that had prevailed at the end of the 1970 crop year. Meanwhile, the refiners had raised the price of refined sugar to reflect the higher cost of the imported sugar. By holding the domestic sugar millers to the 1970 prices, the freeze permitted the refiners to reap a windfall profit. The price of sugar to the final consumer was unaffected, but the distribution of income to producers at the different stages of production was altered to the benefit of the refiners.

The sugar millers were understandably irate over what appeared to be a palpable injustice. Initial petitions to the Cost of Living Council did not result in any remedial action. Although the situation was conceded to be inequitable, it was justified as part of "the luck of the draw" philosophy which underlay the administration of the stabilization program.

This reverence for consistency was ultimately overcome by political realities. Loud and insistent complaints were made to the council by members of the Louisiana Congressional delegation who occupied influential positions on key committees. The Cost of Living Council succumbed to this barrage, and the ruling was modified so that the ceiling price for domestic raw sugar was raised to the same level as imported sugar. However, this action had little or no effect on retail prices, because the higher prices already prevailed for imported raw sugar. This case involved the only modification of a CLC ruling in response to explicit political pressures over the entire course of the freeze.

School lunch prices posed an equally convoluted set of circumstances. During the 1970–71 school year, some schools provided lunches free or at a reduced price to students. This practice was made possible because of subsidies provided by Congressional action. For the school year 1971–72, however, the administration announced that funds available for subsidies would be significantly reduced and eligibility requirements tightened. Some school administrators reacted to this change by maintaining the low price for needy students while raising the price for all other students. The higher price violated the Cost of Living Council's rules. The fact that the price increase was caused by a reduction of the subsidy was disregarded because subsidies were considered as cost factors and an increase in cost caused by a termination of a subsidy could not be passed on.

This ruling caused immediate consternation among school administrators and, within the administration, in the Office of Management and Budget. In reducing the expenditures for school lunch subsidies, OMB expected that the subsidies could continue for the needy students through the additional revenues generated by charging higher prices to the other students. With this alternative blocked, the only remaining option was to replace the subsidy with local funds—a prospect with predictable political consequences. The problem dissolved—to the relief of everyone but OMB officials—when Congress rode to the rescue and provided appropriations for school lunch subsidies that were at approximately the same level as in 1970–71.

Exceptions

Once specific policies were determined, the affected parties could petition for an "exception," or a waiver of the applicable regulation in particular cases. This right was implicit in the section of the Economic Stabilization Act which stated that "orders and regulations may provide for the making of such adjustments as may be necessary to prevent gross inequities."[3] Over the course of the freeze, 2,435 requests for an exception

3. P.L. 91-379 (August 15, 1970), sec. 202.

were received by the regional offices of OEP.[4] Of this total, 49 percent of the requests involved prices, 33 percent wages, and 18 percent rents.

As in other policy areas, statutory guidance for exceptions was extremely limited. Relief could be granted "to prevent gross inequities," but this concept lacked both precision or any amplifying legislative history. As it turned out, over 75 percent of the non-wage requests for exceptions involved situations in which costs had increased before the freeze and the business was precluded from raising prices. This category of cases had by implication been abstractly considered when CLC promulgated the general policy barring cost pass-throughs. In principle, as a result of that general decision, a cost increase clearly did not qualify as a "gross inequity" unless other considerations were present. In this respect, the most powerful claim for an exception was the allegation that, unless an increase in prices was permitted, the petitioner would be forced into bankruptcy.

The binding case concerning the weight to be given to an allegation of impending bankruptcy as a basis for finding the existence of a gross inequity was decided by the full Cost of Living Council. On August 2, 1971, the Kentucky Transport Corporation had agreed to a new labor contract which increased hourly wages from $3.97 to $5.19. On August 13, A & P, Kentucky Transport's sole customer, agreed to an increase in rates to cover the higher labor costs. The agreement was filed with the Interstate Commerce Commission to become effective on August 22, 1971. Because of the imposition of the freeze, the company was caught in a situation in which wages had been increased but the rates it charged A & P were frozen at the existing level. The company alleged that, unless the rate increases that had been negotiated with A & P were allowed to go into effect, it faced imminent bankruptcy.

At the request of OEP, IRS investigated the case and reported that though Kentucky Transport appeared to be well managed, it operated on a narrow profit margin, and the allegation of impending bankruptcy was real. Much of the company's difficulty arose from the fact that it had reduced rates in February 1971 in the expectation that certain economies would be realized, but they had failed to materialize. OEP and the CLC staff recommended that an exception be granted; however, the request was denied by the full council. The denial reflected the contention (1) that Kentucky Transport had contributed to its own economic difficulties and

4. OEP also reported receiving 1,508 requests for exceptions. Many of these requests probably duplicated those submitted to the regional offices, but the exact number is not known.

(2) that by accepting inefficiency as a contributing factor to a determination of a gross inequity a major breach in price control would be created. Impending bankruptcy per se, therefore, was not allowed as a justification for an exception. Instead, the petitioner had the burden of proof in demonstrating that he had not contributed to his difficulties and that all other alternatives had been exhausted. As a footnote to the case, Kentucky Transport avoided bankruptcy when it was granted a loan by A & P on favorable terms.

With this tough line laid down in the Kentucky Transport case, only *five* exceptions were granted during the freeze, and they involved governmental bodies exclusively. For example, in Texas, the state was permitted to put into effect a paid insurance plan when it was shown that many of the employees had canceled individual policies in the expectation that they would be covered by the new plan. Cresco, Iowa, to cite another example, was given permission to raise water and sewerage rates when IRS reported that the town was already in default on bonds to build a new sewage disposal plant.

In handling the other cases, the hard line prevailed. The Ford Motor Company was denied a request to equalize the price of domestically produced Pintos with those produced in Canada and shipped to U.S. dealers. Under CLC rules, the price of the Canadian Pinto could be higher to reflect the cost of the import surcharge. The state of Hawaii was also turned down when it requested relief for the prices of certain consumer goods shipped from the mainland during the course of a prolonged longshoremen's strike. Because the strike had blocked the regular shipping channels, the state government had chartered two ships at higher costs to carry foodstuffs, animal feeds, and paper products to the island from Vancouver, Canada. A special survey by IRS showed that, since only a few shortages had developed, it was not necessary to defray the higher costs to insure an adequate supply of essential goods. Overall, it was apparent that the exceptions route was not an easy way out of the freeze.

The Policy Process

Notwithstanding diversions forced by the pressure for immediate decisions, the process of policy formulation essentially went forth in two stages. First, the Cost of Living Council articulated the broad principles that would determine and define the nature of the freeze and the degree of restraint imposed on the economy. This task was carried out with considerable speed, and, by and large, the resulting policies were internally consistent and afforded equal treatment to different sectors of the economy. In addition, they provided the necessary general principles to guide the public in complying with the stabilization program. This first generation of policies reflected the enthusiasm stimulated by the President's speech when controls were imposed and the simple resolve to be effective. No attempt was made to comprehend or deal with the enormous complexities or individual inequities that could be created by the freeze.

In the second wave of policy determinations, the Cost of Living Council was forced to cope with specific cases, each with its own complications, political pressures, and questions of equity. The technical problems alone were formidable with the limited staff available. In addition, the difficulty of sustaining uniform general policies increased geometrically as the freeze progressed. By the end of the 90 days, the Cost of Living Council was almost running out of thumbs to plug the dike. Nonetheless, in terms of consistency, speed, and responsiveness to the overall objectives of the stabilization program, the policies proved to be adequate to the task. If they engendered significant problems of further adjustment or equity, these would be left to Phase II.

VII

Maintaining the Freeze:
The Tactics of Enforcement

The administrators of a wage-price freeze must deal with difficult problems of enforcement even if the program is relatively simple and receives popular support. Indeed, although there is no standard nomenclature for incomes policies, the different types of policy may be distinguished by reference to the legal authority for enforcement and the strategy adopted to bring about compliance. Thus the distinction between jawboning and controls is essentially a distinction based on the legal authority for enforcement, even though these concepts may involve derivative distinctions concerning the theory and scope of the policy. In general, the more comprehensive the coverage of the incomes policy, the more formal the system of enforcement will have to be.

In this manner, an incomes policy that aims at controlling the price or wage behavior of selected sectors of the economy may be implemented through the use of exhortation or extralegal sanctions. Jawboning, for example, is normally associated with those policies that focus on particular wage or price decisions. In such cases, exhortation and public pressure often suffice to bring about compliance, at least for a limited period. Moreover, large firms or unions that are recalcitrant usually will be vulnerable to extralegal sanctions such as investigation for possible violations of other laws or the revocation of special privileges. When the coverage of an incomes policy is highly comprehensive, however, legal sanctions, or the threat of legal sanctions, may have to be employed to attain an acceptable level of compliance. Only so much time and energy can be expended in jawboning and in mustering particular extralegal sanctions. In the absence of a system of enforcement, the mere identification of violations may undermine public confidence in the program. When virtually universal controls are imposed, as was the case in August 1971, some formal sanctions are necessary to provide the assurance of equity even though primary reliance might be placed on other means for obtaining compliance.

Once a formal enforcement program is adopted, it is subject to the constraints applicable to any system for securing compliance. The program must be founded on the operational premise that the overwhelming majority of people will conform voluntarily to the law and that only a small proportion of the violators will or can be caught and successfully prosecuted. Consequently, a general strategy of enforcement should encourage voluntary compliance while convincing potential violators that some of them will be identified, apprehended, and subjected to sanctions.

Such considerations are particularly relevant to the development of an enforcement strategy for a wage-price freeze. The objective of a freeze is not and cannot be to control every price or wage rate. Rather, the goal is to assure that the general level of prices and wages does not rise perceptibly. It is of little significance when the price of peanut butter rises in a supermarket in Keokuk, Iowa; but it is significant when the price of entire categories of goods rises throughout the country. The simple objectives of a freeze do not warrant an extensive enforcement apparatus. On the other hand, securing voluntary compliance depends to some degree on making the public feel that everyone will be treated equally and that enforcement will be comprehensive and even-handed. These conflicting considerations may be accommodated by adopting comprehensive coverage while applying sanctions selectively in order to maximize the public visibility, or spill-over effects, of each enforcement action. This optimizing approach can be perilous, however, because the establishment of comprehensive coverage will engender pressures to extend and augment enforcement efforts. Nonetheless, to the extent that a wage-price freeze is of short duration, it may be possible to perform this balancing act without undermining the integrity of the program.

The Search for Sanctions

Within this framework, several pragmatic factors gave ultimate shape to the enforcement program developed during the freeze. First, the President had explicitly stated his intent to avoid a "huge bureaucracy" in the administration of the economic stabilization program. This antipathy toward bureaucracy implied a limited commitment of personnel to enforcement activities or the verification of compliance in the field. Instead, primary emphasis was placed on voluntary compliance. The image cultivated was one of businessmen, landlords, and employees forthrightly denying themselves personal gain in the name of the national interest, as contrasted to one of cadres of accountants poring over ledger books and payroll stubs to bring malefactors to justice.

Second, the Economic Stabilization Act did not include a complete or particularly formidable arsenal of legal procedures and sanctions. The amendments of 1971 did authorize both civil penalties and criminal fines for violation of the freeze. The administering agency could ask the Justice Department to seek an injunction in federal court to restrain violators. In addition, violations could lead to fines up to $5,000. The limited amount of the maximum fine permissible under the law made criminal charges unattractive as an enforcement technique, however, particularly in view of the lengthy legal proceedings that were generally necessary to obtain a criminal conviction.

In order to magnify the effectiveness of the criminal penalties, active consideration was given to the possibility of seeking a $5,000 fine for each individual infraction of the law—e.g., a $5,000 fine would be levied for each can of peas that was sold above the ceiling price rather than one $5,000 fine for the act of setting a price above the ceiling. The Justice Department ruled that this approach could not be sustained in the courts, and it was dropped as an alternative. In fact, civil proceedings and the injunction were used exclusively during the freeze.

Whether civil or criminal remedies were sought, several legal hurdles had to be overcome. Because the Economic Stabilization Act was essentially an exercise in political tactics by Congress, it did not include the normal powers necessary for effective enforcement. Most important, the Internal Revenue Service did not have subpoena power under the statute when investigating possible violations of the freeze. Consequently, an alleged violator could refuse to provide records that were necessary to build a credible case. When records were withheld—and it did occur during the freeze—the Justice Department was forced to resort to cumbersome and time-consuming "discovery procedures." At the same time, the absence of any statutory provisions establishing the administrative powers of the enforcement agency meant that initial findings and decisions were subject to review de novo by the federal district courts. Normally, the courts limit their review of the actions of a regulatory agency to a review of an administrative record, with the agency's determination upheld if there is substantial evidence to support it. The fact that the Economic Stabilization Act was silent on these administrative procedures and powers meant that extended delays could be expected in obtaining decisions as a consequence of the de novo proceedings in the courts. These delays could be particularly important in the context of a 90-day freeze.

In fact, such delays did develop and undermined the enforcement program in some cases involving probable violation by a class of litigants. This happened when steps were taken to bring about compliance with respect to increases in teachers' salaries and the price of tickets for sporting events.[1] In both instances, the respondents generally had adopted an adversary position toward the policies and rulings of the Cost of Living Council.

The procedural requirements for seeking criminal remedies for violations and the inherent limitations of an injunction, which merely restrained a seller from charging illegal prices, stimulated an exploration of other possible sanctions. Extensive legal research was carried out to determine whether the government could also seek restitution for violations of the law prior to the issuance of an injunction. Initially, it was determined that the statute did not permit the government to seek this remedy. However, the Justice Department subsequently revised its opinion and recommended that restitution be sought on the grounds that a court of equity could fashion any remedy to do justice, including the return of overpayments. This position was accepted by the federal courts in *United States* v. *Lieb*.[2] There was also a possibility that restitution could be gained through private suits, but, as far as is known, no suits for recovery of overcharges were ever filed by private parties during the freeze.

Acute limitations of time further conditioned the nature of the enforcement program. Administratively, the wage-price freeze began from a standing start on the evening of August 15, 1971. The development of an elaborate system of enforcement would have required the recruitment, training, and deployment of large numbers of personnel. Despite the most strenuous efforts, it was probably impossible to launch a comprehensive

1. In the case of teachers' pay and ticket prices the Justice Department filed suits in the federal courts to remedy alleged violations of the freeze. Neither issue was resolved by the end of the freeze.

The teachers' situation was complicated by the fact that several suits and countersuits were filed in different U.S. district courts. For example: *U.S.* v. *Jefferson Parish School Board* (New Orleans), September 23, 1971; *California Teachers Association* v. *Cost of Living Council* (Los Angeles), October 26, 1971.

U.S. v. *The Five Smiths Inc.* (Atlanta), September 27, 1971, involved the Atlanta Falcons football team.

2. *United States* v. *Lieb*, 333 F. Supp. 424 (W.D. Tex. 1971). This decision was affirmed by the Temporary Emergency Court of Appeals, 462 F.2d 1161 (TECA, No. 5-1, 1972).

system of enforcement over the duration of the freeze. To be sure, the establishment of a compliance force and procedures could move ahead with maximum speed on the assumption that these bureaucratic tools would be necessary in the post-freeze period. Because the nature and scope of the Phase II program could not be easily predicted during the first month of the freeze, however, the expansion of a compliance force under these circumstances would require a high degree of executive daring. To make matters worse, no appropriations were available for the direct funding of the stabilization program. Modest amounts of financial resources could be extracted from existing budgets, but it was probably illegal or infeasible to commandeer large sums of money under the terms of existing appropriations legislation.[3]

Lastly, no sensible enforcement program could be devised until the rules to be enforced were themselves created. On August 15 there were no detailed policies governing the freeze, and the laborious task of drafting rules and regulations still lay ahead.

Developing an Enforcement Strategy

Both the theory of enforcement and the practical considerations meant that voluntary compliance buttressed by unbounded exhortation would be the dominant method for gaining public adherence to the wage-price freeze. The initial urgings to support the freeze came from the President himself and subsequently were echoed by various Cabinet officers, the President's consumer adviser, and private associations such as the U.S. Chamber of Commerce. Inevitably, bumper stickers and other paraphernalia of economic patriotism appeared to promote acceptance of and compliance with the stabilization program. But even the most dedicated optimist recognized that voluntary compliance and exhortation, by themselves, would not be sufficient to insure effective enforcement of the freeze, particularly as the initial euphoria was dissipated. Thus efforts to cultivate voluntary compliance were soon supplemented by more tangible methods

3. Because of time limitations, the Cost of Living Council did not have its own appropriations. Personnel costs were assumed by the agencies that provided the personnel on loan to CLC and the other agencies involved in the freeze. Additional costs were defrayed from a special fund in the Treasury Department, financed by the profits from the sale of foreign exchange.

of enforcement, such as jawboning, the threat of legal action, and, in a few cases, the initiation of court proceedings.

Information

The initial widespread disposition to comply voluntarily with the wage-price freeze could be reinforced, it was felt, through rapid and unambiguous dissemination of rules and regulations. At the outset of the freeze, therefore, great emphasis was placed on relatively simple statements of policy that could be conveyed rapidly and concisely to the public. As noted above, the question-and-answer format was used extensively to promote public understanding. Also, simplicity and clarity were given considerable weight in the process of policy formulation even though the development of relatively simple rules would ignore or override special circumstances that otherwise merited attention.

For example, in many cases the price of certain commodities sold in supermarkets, such as coffee, soap, and canned goods, was unrealistically low because a promotional sale had been in effect in the period immediately preceding the freeze. Economic and equity considerations dictated that special rules should be developed to provide for alternate base periods for the calculation of the ceiling price. The Cost of Living Council, however, believed that this approach would be difficult to comprehend and would introduce major complications into the compliance system. Therefore no relief was offered, and the ceiling price was held to the price that prevailed in the 30-day base period preceding the freeze, whether or not it reflected special promotional discounts. As the freeze progressed, the enormous complexity of the economy overrode the desire for simplicity. Thus regulations covering matters such as seasonality, commercial and financial leases, used cars, and insurance involved inherent complexity that reduced public understanding and created significant problems of compliance.

The need for unambiguous, readily accessible information for the public also was a central consideration in fashioning policies governing the posting of ceiling prices. The basic requirement concerning the availability of ceiling price lists was laid down in Executive Order 11615 that instituted the freeze. Section 1 of the order stated that: "Each person engaged in the business of selling or providing commodities or services shall maintain available for public inspection a record of the highest prices or rents charged for such or similar commodities or services during the 30-day period ending August 14, 1971."

On October 4, 1971, the Cost of Living Council issued a policy statement requiring all businesses to establish and maintain ceiling price lists on an item-by-item basis. The policy further provided that the price lists were to be made available at each place of business, including each one operated by multi-establishment firms such as retail chains. When a customer questioned a ceiling price, the seller was encouraged but not required to reveal his supporting records. These records were viewed as proprietary information and therefore were not available for public inspection except at the option of the seller. However, the seller was required to reveal all the lists and supporting records to federal personnel responsible for investigating complaints.

When this policy was promulgated, it precipitated a flood of protests from large retail establishments and the national retail trade associations. The protests focused on both the form of the list and the requirement itself. The retailers alleged that the preparation of the list was extremely complex and costly, that the list would be difficult, if not impossible, to maintain, and that it was impractical to require prices on an item-by-item basis. Extensive discussions were held with representatives of the various trade associations to explain the necessity for, and the nature of, the posting requirement. The issue became more sensitive when Ralph Nader, the consumer advocate, wrote to the Cost of Living Council to ask what had been done to implement the posting requirement specified in the executive order.

The Cost of Living Council sought to balance the complaints of the retailers against the needs of the program. The resulting accommodation was less than satisfactory. The requirement calling for the maintenance and public availability of an item-by-item list of prices was retained; but the deadline for the mandatory availability of the list was extended to November 1, 1971. In the interim, retailers were permitted to utilize an alternate procedure. Under this procedure, the seller was required to post at least one sign in a prominent place in the store and at each cash register to explain to the customer the availability of a list of ceiling prices upon request. If the price information was not immediately available in the store, a form letter was to be provided by the store to inform the customer of the ceiling price of the item at issue.

Although this procedure was acceptable to the retailers, it precipitated sharp criticism from various "watchdog groups" that had been organized in major cities across the country. Many of these watchdog groups had been inspired by trade unions ostensibly to insure the uniform application of the freeze to wages and prices. In several cities, particularly New York, these organizations aggressively monitored prices and, when price lists were not available, reported this omission with considerable clamor.

The announcement on October 7 of the plans for Phase II, the post-freeze stabilization program, further complicated the situation. It was clear that the Price Commission envisioned for Phase II would have to relax the freeze and permit price movements on the basis of some criteria or formulae. The nature of these criteria or formulae would determine, in a large measure, the form and magnitude of the posting requirement. At this stage, though, the members of the Price Commission were still to be selected and the commission's standards yet to be developed. It was not logical to require sellers to develop and post lists that would soon be obsolete. This anomaly was accentuated by the fact that only two weeks remained between the November 1 deadline for the posting of the lists and November 14 when Phase II would commence. Under these circumstances, the Cost of Living Council beat what it hoped would be a quiet retreat. A few days before the November 1 deadline, CLC suspended the requirement calling for the mandatory posting of ceiling price lists at each place of business and instead permitted the continuance of the interim procedure.

This abortive approach to the posting of price lists did not advance compliance with the program. Aside from operational difficulties, the absence of a satisfactory arrangement for conveying ceiling price information to the public created a vulnerability that could be exploited by those who opposed the program on other grounds.

Pressure Tactics

Although heavy emphasis was placed on voluntary compliance, the Cost of Living Council also had a range of pressure tactics that were used on a selective basis. Probably the most effective and easily utilized tactic was jawboning: the expression of censure by high government officials in order to mobilize public opinion against an apparent violator. Jawboning would be most effective during the early stages of the freeze when public acceptance of the economic stabilization program was at a peak and observers were assessing the extent of the administration's commitment to the effort. When jawboning brought about compliance, confidence in the program rose, and the government's success set an example to dissuade other potential transgressors.

The effectiveness of jawboning as a tactic was abetted by a fortuitous set of circumstances which involved the Cost of Living Council with two causes célèbres early in the freeze. As noted above, the Department of Defense and the state of Texas had each acted in clear noncompliance with the freeze by approving wage increases to take effect after August 15. In both cases, the pay increases were rescinded following well-publicized confrontations with Secretary of the Treasury Connally. These incidents served to demonstrate the firm intention to enforce the freeze regardless of the sensitivities involved. It is interesting to note that thereafter the Department of Defense and Texas state officials checked beforehand with the Cost of Living Council staff before initiating any action which appeared to be remotely related to the conditions of the freeze.

For some kinds of economic activity, exhortation and jawboning were the only available means of influence. This was true in the case of interest and dividends. Neither of these forms of income was subject to controls under the terms of the Economic Stabilization Act. Consequently, control could be achieved only through extralegal techniques. Intensive persuasion was the primary element in the government's strategy for both interest and dividends. The Secretary of the Treasury sent letters to about 40,000 financial institutions to ask them to hold the line on interest charges. Similarly, the Secretary of Commerce dispatched telegrams to the chief executives of the 1,250 largest corporations of the country to ask that they follow the dividend guidelines that had been adopted by the Cost of Living Council. According to reports provided by the Secretary of Commerce to the Cost of Living Council, every company contacted agreed to cooperate with the stabilization program.

No overt violation of the hold-the-line request on interest rates came to the attention of the Cost of Living Council during the freeze. Doubtless there were some individual cases in which interest charges were increased; however, the major categories of interest rates, in fact, declined steadily throughout the freeze.[4]

The problem of control was more complicated in dealing with dividends. According to reports received from the various financial services during the freeze, the overwhelming proportion of American corporations

4. See p. 40, n. 6, for a discussion of changes in interest rates during the freeze.

followed dividend practices that were consistent with the standards promulgated by the Cost of Living Council. For many corporations, the admonition to keep dividends at prior levels provided a justification for actions that were in the firm's self-interest. By citing the guidelines, firms that might otherwise have felt obliged to increase dividends could maintain them at the previous rate and retain the earnings. In some cases, however, dividend payments rose because individual firms had a seasonal pattern of dividends which called for increased payments during the freeze or were obliged by legal provisions to distribute a certain proportion of earnings. In a few reported instances, firms willfully ignored the dividend guidelines.

The glare of publicity in a few known instances of willful disregard caused the CLC staff to drop their tolerant approach toward dividends. In early September 1971, the *Wall Street Journal* published a story reporting that six small- or medium-sized companies had increased their dividend payments in apparent contravention of the hold-the-line policy. This story precipitated an animated discussion in the Cost of Living Council. Despite the obvious reluctance of the Secretary of Commerce, it was decided that the chief executive of each of the companies named in the *Journal* story would be sent a telegram asking that he come to Washington in the next 48 hours to discuss his action with a subcommittee of the council. The telegrams were made public, focusing national attention on the cases.

Stunned at their newly found notoriety, the chief executives of the designated companies dutifully traveled to Washington to meet with the Chairman of the Council of Economic Advisers (who also served as Vice-Chairman of CLC), the Secretary of Commerce, and the Executive Director of the Cost of Living Council. During the meeting, the discourse was generally polite and restrained. Paul McCracken, the Chairman of CEA, indicated the importance of attaining complete compliance with the President's request to limit dividends in view of the curbs that had been placed on increases in wages, prices, and rents. With one exception, each of the executives indicated a willingness to accept any reasonable remedy for his actions. Only one company, the Florida Telephone Corporation, resisted the government's blandishments. Both the president and the attorney of the firm rejected the implication that their corporation had committed any illegality or impropriety, and they attacked the summons to Washington as an improper exercise of power.

With each of the other companies, remedies were worked out which brought actual or symbolic compliance with the freeze on dividends. Those companies that had merely announced their intention to raise dividends rescinded these announcements. Those companies that had already declared an increase in dividends by action of the board of directors and who were thus legally bound, agreed to offset this increase by an equivalent reduction of the "normal" dividend in the succeeding quarter.

Only in the case of the Florida Telephone Corporation was additional leverage necessary. Here, contacts were made by administration officials with members of the financial community and large customers of the company who presumably could exert some pressure on management. The president of the firm, who by circumstance or habit cast himself in the role of a sturdy individualist, finally agreed to offset the dividend increase in the subsequent quarter if the dividend guidelines were still in effect at that time. The CLC chairman issued a statement which expressed satisfaction over the disposition of each of the cases.

Immediately following this interplay with the six companies, the Cost of Living Council established a systematic program for monitoring dividend payments and following up on apparent violations of the CLC guidelines. With the help of Securities and Exchange Commission personnel, each dividend payment announced by individual firms during the remaining period of the freeze was reviewed in the light of the company's past dividend record. If an apparent infraction was identified, a telegram requesting additional information was sent to the company by CLC's Executive Director. When further analysis revealed that a dividend payment was, in fact, in excess of the voluntary standards, a second telegram was sent by the Chairman of the Cost of Living Council. This communication requested that the company take steps to roll back the dividend to an acceptable level or pledge that it would offset the extra payment in subsequent periods. In the event that this request did not bring about compliance, the council publicly announced that the company was in violation of the spirit of the stabilization program. Other indirect methods of exercising pressure on the company were sometimes sought, depending upon the circumstances.

The dividend compliance program appeared to be highly successful. In the three-month period of the freeze, only a handful of apparent violators were identified.[5] In almost every case, there was some technical justification for the increase in dividends, or the company agreed to an acceptable remedy. To be sure, such widespread compliance could be considered as a

5. No exact tally was kept, but the number of alleged violators of the dividends guidelines was probably less than fifty.

measure of business support for the stabilization program. At a more general level, however, this record of compliance demonstrated that the task of control was facilitated when there was comprehensive, uniform information available on a regular basis and when the economic incentives were such that it was to the advantage of the economic unit to comply with the policies of the program.

Legal Action

When appeals for voluntary compliance or jawboning failed, legal sanctions authorized by the Economic Stabilization Act could be exercised, but for two reasons this step was viewed as a risky alternative. First, the initiation of court proceedings might elicit challenges on constitutional grounds or because of the procedural deficiencies of the statute. There was agreement by Justice Department and Cost of Living Council lawyers that the program was highly vulnerable to legal tests. Second, any legal proceedings could be prolonged and indecisive. As indicated above, the Cost of Living Council did not have explicit administrative procedures affording the litigant due process. Therefore, each case would be tried de novo in the federal district court where the complaint was lodged. Moreover, even if the government was sustained by the district court, there was the right of appeal. In the interim, experience indicated that there were likely to be different opinions on the same factual circumstances among different district courts. Legal proceedings were therefore likely to create ambiguities during the period of the freeze rather than provide an effective instrument of enforcement.

For these reasons, the *threat* of legal sanctions was the preferred technique rather than the actual initiation of court proceedings. As the procedures for enforcement were gradually elaborated, emphasis was placed upon the manipulation of such threats of legal action rather than actual court suits. When an infraction was identified, initial discussions were held by IRS with the party to request voluntary compliance. In the large majority of cases compliance was forthcoming. If the violator was unwilling to comply, a formal investigation was initiated. The fact that the initial investigation was conducted by IRS agents had an implicit coercive effect because of the general reputation of the agency. When the file was prepared, it was forwarded to the OEP regional office where it was further reviewed by OEP staff and an Assistant U.S. Attorney. If the Assistant

U.S. Attorney sustained a recommendation of court action, the alleged violator was sent a "last chance" telegram. Formal legal action was taken only if the party still maintained an uncompromising position. Approximately 200 "last chance" letters were sent to alleged violators, and legal measures were actually initiated by the government in 8 cases.

The most consequential cases in which the threat of legal action induced compliance involved a group of railroads in Georgia and several major distributors of propane gas located in various parts of the country. In the Georgia case, the railroads had increased rates with the approval of the State Railroad Commission. This approval came after a protracted procedure whereby requests first had to be made to the Interstate Commerce Commission and then were subject to further review and approval by the state commission. Even though the railroads had filed their request much earlier, the actual timing of the rate increase was such that it was prohibited under the terms of the freeze. Contacts were made with the railroads through the OEP regional office in Atlanta and high officials of the Department of Transportation. The OEP regional director indicated that unless compliance was forthcoming within 48 hours, the government would file suit for an injunction. Confronted with this prospect, the railroads quickly complied, disclaiming any intention to violate the regulations governing the freeze.

In the propane case, some major distributors had raised their prices, justifying the action on the grounds that this action was permitted by the seasonality rule. After examining the facts, the OEP staff concluded that the seasonality rule was inapplicable and therefore that the price increase was illegal. When the gas companies balked at rescinding the increase, legal action was threatened. Consequently, one of the major companies, Wanda Petroleum, reversed its position, and within a few days the other firms followed.

The government filed suits against the violators in only eight cases.[6] Five of these cases pertained to rent, two concerned salary increases instituted by local school boards in apparent violation of the Cost of Living Council regulations, and one involved a price increase for sports tickets. None of the suits were important to the overall economic effectiveness of the freeze. Instead, they were largely symbolic of the government's willingness to enforce the stabilization program in a decisive, comprehensive

6. Memorandum from L. Patrick Gray III, Assistant Attorney General, to Donald Rumsfeld, Director of the Cost of Living Council, December 22, 1971.

manner. The rent decisions, in particular, catered to public sentiment. By moving against violators of the rent regulations, the Cost of Living Council could demonstrate its concern for individuals as contrasted to corporate entities. And for reasons that are evidently rooted in the psyche of landlords, rent violations engendered the greatest number of cases in which the alleged violator remained adamant.

The teacher salary cases were part of the continued maneuvering between the Cost of Living Council and the teacher organizations. Because violations involving teachers appeared to be widespread, the three cases were instituted primarily to diminish other school boards' enthusiasm for instituting salary increases during the freeze.

Similar considerations contributed to perhaps the most complicated legal proceeding arising during the freeze. This involved a complaint filed against the Atlanta Falcons professional football club. Under the terms of the "transaction" rule, it was determined that the prices charged for attendance at athletic events could not be increased above the level that prevailed during the base period, and for some sports "base period" meant the past season, during the fall and winter. Even though tickets for the forthcoming season had been sold *before* August 15, 1971, at a higher price, CLC insisted on last season's prices as a ceiling. This ruling had the greatest impact on professional football and hockey, which were commencing their regular seasons during the 90-day freeze period. Some of the teams agreed to roll back the ticket price increases and to adopt procedures to provide refunds to the buyers. In 40 different cases, however, the teams were unwilling to comply, and a test case was initiated early in the freeze against the Atlanta Falcons football team. Significantly, the Falcons played five of their six home games during the 90-day period and would incur a heavy loss of revenue if they acquiesced in the request for a rollback in ticket prices. As a practical matter, the longer the case was drawn out, the less likely that any decision would result in a constructive remedy.[7]

The tactical plan for gaining compliance clearly reflected the theoretical and practical considerations associated with the wage-price freeze. The comprehensive scope of the stabilization program, the nature of the substantive policies, and the limited resources available for enforcement activities all dictated that the greatest emphasis should be given to exhorta-

7. The Falcons case, *United States* v. *The Five Smiths Inc.*, had not been settled by early 1973. However, in a similar case, *University of Southern California* v. *Cost of Living Council*, 342 F. Supp. 606 (TECA, No. 9-1, 1972), the position of the government was sustained. For a discussion of this case, see p. 120.

tion and voluntary compliance. Continued attention would be focused on public relations and the widespread dissemination of the regulations governing the freeze. Although some independent monitoring was carried out by the IRS, complaints by the public were the primary method for identifying alleged violations. Violators were initially subject to persuasion and pressure, depending upon their vulnerability to each approach. The threat of legal action was brandished with some frequency, but court proceedings were rarely initiated, and then only to show firmness against notorious violations or to provide a dramatic example. By combining the presumption of compliance with the capacity for inflicting public retribution the government hoped to preserve the effectiveness of the freeze through the 90-day period.

VIII

The Record of Compliance

The most relevant measure of compliance in economic terms is the performance of wages and prices during the freeze period. For an assessment of the symbolic and political dimensions of compliance, the administrative record should provide some insight into the effectiveness of the freeze. If the administrative machinery established by the Cost of Living Council was inundated by complaints, and if these complaints accumulated without constructive disposition, then the political success of the program would be doubtful, just as a rising price level during the freeze would signal economic failure.

Price and Wage Behavior

Although the freeze nominally aimed at repressing individual wage and price increases, its operational objective was to restrain the upward movement of wages and prices in general. The best measures of changes in the general level of prices during the freeze are provided by the consumer price index and the wholesale price index prepared by the Bureau of Labor Statistics (BLS). Certain caveats should be noted, however, in using these indexes to assess the freeze. Two significant categories of goods—raw agricultural products and imported finished goods—were not subject to controls and could fluctuate in response to market forces. In addition, the specific policies governing the freeze did permit price increases under three general circumstances: when the price of a commodity in the 30-day base period was lower than the price that had been in effect on May 25, 1970; when there were well-established seasonal fluctuations in price; or when goods were directly subject to an import surcharge. Moreover, the transaction rule permitted the price charged by a given seller for a particular good to rise to the level reached by the upper 10 percent of his sales in the base period.

The indexes themselves also have deficiencies for purposes of isolating the effect of the freeze. For certain items, prices are not reported every month, and so a price increase recorded during the freeze may have taken place in a month prior to the freeze. In addition, the consumer price index covers taxes, interest, and related items that were not considered to be "prices" for the purposes of the stabilization program.[1] Special analyses by the BLS of data for particular categories of goods permit a more refined evaluation, but these corrections do not provide a measure that is exactly coextensive with the scope of the program.

Within these limitations, the major price indexes showed a marked deceleration during the freeze period. As indicated in Table 2, the consumer price index rose at an annual rate of 1.6 percent between August and November 1971, as contrasted to 4.0 percent in the six months preceding the freeze. The decline in the rate of increase in the wholesale price index was even more dramatic. During the six months prior to the freeze, wholesale prices had risen at a 4.9 percent annual rate; once the freeze was imposed, the index actually declined at an annual rate of almost 0.4 percent. While the consumer index edged up in small increments, the wholesale index showed a wider range of movement, dropping 0.4 percentage point in September, then increasing by 0.2 percentage point in October and again by 0.1 percentage point in November.

The overall record of price performance, and hence compliance, appears further improved upon identification of those components of the increase in the consumer index that can be explained by BLS procedures or the rules governing the freeze. Approximately one-fifth of the increase in the consumer index between August and September was attributable to price changes that had taken place before August 15. Imports were responsible for 2.5 percent of the increase in the September index. Another 10 percent of the increase was explained by hikes in college tuition charges that had been approved by the Cost of Living Council in the early stage of the program.[2] Similarly, about 50 percent of the increase in the October index reflected changes in the prices of items exempt from the freeze, such as food or new cars.[3] Half the upward movement of the consumer index between October and November could be attributed to further increases in the prices of exempt commodities.[4]

1. The relationship between the coverage of the freeze and the consumer price index is discussed in U.S. Department of Labor News Release 71-490, September 5, 1971. A related discussion of the wholesale price index appears in USDL News Release 71-509, September 22, 1971.

2. USDL News Release 71-562, October 22, 1971, p. 4.

3. USDL News Release 71-616, November 19, 1971, p. 5.

4. USDL News Release 71-689, December 22, 1971, p. 3.

The assessment of general compliance with the freeze is not seriously modified by an examination of the major product categories in each of the indexes. The price levels for all components of the wholesale index presented in Table 2 remained the same or declined, with the exception of food (which encompassed raw agricultural products that were outside the freeze) and crude materials (including minerals) whose prices had some latitude under the operation of the May 25 rule. The largest increases in the consumer index were registered by foods, nondurable goods, services, and rent. Many food prices were of course exempt, and some of the increase in the price of services and rents had occurred before the freeze.

The "softest" areas of compliance appeared to be insurance and finance in the services category and apparel within the nondurable goods category. Insurance and finance includes mortgage interest charges whose decline contributed to the stability of the index for this category in the six months preceding the freeze. Nonetheless, the fact that the index for insurance and finance increased sharply during the freeze flagged insurance rates as a problem category. Increases in insurance rates were permitted if a "substantial volume of transactions" had taken place for existing policies in the base period; however, this permissive approach may have been generalized to all policies without justification in the absence of specific guidance or close monitoring by CLC. Similarly, some of the increase in apparel prices may have been accommodated by the seasonality rule. The more reasonable inference is that noncompliance, whether through ignorance or intent, was sufficiently widespread to affect the price level for these commodities.

Another approach to measuring the extent of compliance with the freeze is to examine the behavior of individual prices in the consumer index. In view of the stringent rules governing the freeze, an overwhelming proportion of the prices could be expected to remain constant or decline. In fact, a special BLS analysis of 98,000 individual prices collected on a monthly basis showed that approximately 79 percent of the prices remained constant, 10 percent declined, and 11 percent increased during the September to November period. Of the prices that did rise, the largest proportion was in the "food at home" category which included the exempt raw agricultural products.[5]

Similar data are not available for the wholesale index. However, some indication of the nature and extent of individual wholesale price move-

5. Compiled from USDL News Releases 71-562 and 71-616.

Table 2. *Prices and Wages during and before the Freeze*
Seasonally adjusted percentage of base figure (1967 = 100)

Description	Price or wage index during freeze period (August–November 1971)				Percentage change in price or wage index (annual rate)	
	August	September	October	November	August–November 1971	Six months prior to freeze
Consumer prices						
All items	122.1	122.2	122.4	122.6	1.6	4.0
Food	119.2	118.9	118.9	119.7	1.7	5.2
Commodities	118.1	118.1	118.2	118.4	1.0	4.0
Commodities, less food	117.5	117.5	117.5	117.5	0	3.5
Durables	117.0	116.9	116.7	116.8	−0.7	3.0
Nondurables	118.4	118.5	118.7	118.9	1.7	4.2
Apparel	120.2	120.5	121.0	121.1	3.0	2.0
All services[a]	129.4	129.9	130.0	130.4	3.1	4.5
Medical care	130.0	130.4	129.6	129.7	−0.9	4.6
Insurance and finance	139.0	139.6	140.1	140.9	5.6	−0.7
Rent[a]	115.8	116.1	116.4	116.6	2.8	3.9

Wholesale prices

All items^b	115.1	114.7	114.9	115.0	−0.3	4.9
Farm products, processed foods, feeds^b	114.7	113.3	114.6	115.0	1.0	3.0
Industrial commodities	115.3	115.2	115.0	115.1	−0.7	5.6
Consumer finished goods, except food	111.7	111.6	111.3	111.4	−1.1	1.7
Durables	111.9	111.2	110.6	110.7	−4.4	2.7
Nondurables	111.7	111.8	111.7	111.7	0	1.6
Producer finished goods	117.6	117.5	117.0	116.8	−2.7	3.5
Intermediate goods	116.1	116.1	115.9	115.8	−1.0	7.5
Crude materials	123.0	123.2	123.6	123.3	1.0	3.3
Manufactured goods	115.0	114.8	114.6	114.6	−1.4	5.4
Average hourly earnings^c						
Private non-farm economy	130.9	131.3	131.4	131.6	2.2	6.7
Manufacturing	128.8	129.1	129.1	129.0	0.6	6.2

Sources: Price data from the consumer index and the wholesale index published monthly by the Bureau of Labor Statistics; wage index derived from data in the relevant issues of *Employment and Earnings*, Vol. 18 (February 1972), p. 113.

a. No seasonal adjustments made for services or rent.

b. BLS does not publish seasonally adjusted indexes of the wholesale prices of industrial commodities and farm products, processed foods, and feeds; nor does the Bureau incorporate seasonal adjustments in the all-items index. The seasonally adjusted figures offered for these categories in this table were calculated by applying to the unadjusted indexes seasonal factors separately provided by BLS.

c. Adjusted for inter-industry shifts and overtime in manufacturing only.

ments can be obtained by examining the behavior during the freeze of index components, other than farm products, at the four-digit level of the Census industrial classification system (which includes specific commodities such as butter, paperboard, cement, and so forth). Such an analysis of price changes between August and November shows that 41 percent of 251 four-digit categories remained constant, 30 percent declined, and 29 percent increased. In only a few cases was the higher price level in November below the level that had prevailed in May 1970—a circumstance that may have permitted "legal" increases under the terms of the Economic Stabilization Act.[6] Changes in the indexes for four-digit categories are not the same as changes in individual prices; nonetheless, these data do indicate a greater dispersion of wholesale price movements than of consumer price movements, and a significant proportion of wholesale prices did increase during the freeze.

The superior performance of the wholesale index for all items, as contrasted to the consumer index, thus appears to reflect the greater incidence and magnitude of price *reductions* rather than simple compliance with the terms of the freeze. For six months prior to the freeze, all major categories on the wholesale index had been moving upward. The explanation for the relatively high incidence of wholesale price reductions between August and November is not readily apparent, but three considerations offer a plausible interpretation of this development.

First, wholesale commodities generally are purchased by firms rather than individual consumers. Firms could be expected to have better information concerning the meaning of the rules of the freeze and to apply these rules expeditiously to their purchases. Good information was particularly important in interpreting the critical "transaction rule" and may have resulted in the rollback of published prices in some cases.

Second, in some cases the wholesale index is derived from published prices rather than transaction prices, and it is possible that many firms reacted to the freeze by reducing published prices to a level closer to lower transaction prices.[7] The fact that considerable excess capacity existed in the economy in August 1971 lends some credence to this judgment.

6. BLS, *Wholesale Prices and Price Indexes for May 1970* (1970), *August 1971* (1972), and *November 1971* (1972). The four-digit categories that rose significantly but that still stayed below the index for May 1970 included cutting tools and accessories and other types of machinery.

7. For an analysis of the relationship between published wholesale prices and actual transaction prices, see George J. Stigler and James K. Kindahl, *The Behavior of Industrial Prices* (Columbia University Press for the National Bureau of Economic Research, 1970).

Third, large producers of consumer goods may have renegotiated downward the prices charged by suppliers when the price of the final good was frozen and increased costs could not be passed along to the consumer. One automobile manufacturer, for example, stated that the company actively renegotiated the prices charged by its suppliers when the Cost of Living Council held prices of the 1972 models to the 1971 levels. In this manner, a firm with monopsony power could take steps to redistribute the costs of the freeze.

Wage developments in the August–November period also indicated general compliance with the stabilization program. Specific wage rate data are not available, but the BLS index of average hourly earnings corrected for inter-industry shifts and overtime in manufacturing provides a fair approximation of wage rates for the economy as a whole. As shown in Table 2, the index of average hourly earnings for employees in manufacturing came to a virtual halt between August and November, rising at an annual rate of 0.6 percent. This slight increase contrasted with a 6.2 percent annual rate in the previous six months. Average hourly earnings for the private non-farm economy, adjusted for inter-industry shifts and overtime in maufacturing only, increased by 2.2 percent during the freeze, a sharp drop from the 6.7 percent annual rate that prevailed between February and August 1971.

Much of the increase in average hourly earnings that did take place during the freeze occurred in contract construction and transportation and public utilities. Although increases in actual wage rates cannot be specifically identified, CLC rules did permit upward adjustments in construction wages. In many cases, wage increases had been negotiated for construction workers before the freeze but had been placed in escrow pending approval by the Construction Industry Stabilization Committee. When the approval was granted, CLC permitted the increases retroactive to the effective date of the union-management agreement and continuing through the freeze period.

Complaints and Violations

An additional measure of compliance with the stabilization program is provided by an analysis of complaints and other allegations of violations. These complaints, of course, do not provide a comprehensive or objective appraisal of the stabilization effort. But they may help to identify problem areas and to gauge the perception of the program by the public.

Critics of the stabilization effort maintained that the incidence of complaints was a misleading index of administrative performance. As this reasoning went, the enforcement machinery during the freeze was so insubstantial that the number of reports of alleged violations was not an accurate proxy for the effectiveness of the compliance program. Because remedial action on complaints was likely to be slow and/or inconclusive, many violations were never reported to IRS and therefore were not recorded.

Though this argument of prospective futility may have a superficial attractiveness, it is without serious merit. Tautologically, it implies that *any* level of formal complaints would be a measure of non-performance rather than compliance. In addition, although there is no way of determining how each and every employer, worker, seller, and consumer in the country acted and felt, the various BLS estimates of the diffusion of price movements in September–November 1971 do not support a presumption of endemic violations. Public opinion polls taken during the freeze strongly indicate that most people accepted the program and that this acceptance was more likely to be translated into a willingness to register complaints than to ignore violations on the grounds that the program was an administrative nullity.[8]

During the 90-day period, OEP and IRS received 46,387 complaints.[9] Undoubtedly, large numbers of additional complaints were made but were not recorded because of vagueness or the unwillingness of the complainant to put the matter in writing. The best available measure of specific interest in the application of the freeze is the number of inquiries that were received by IRS and OEP. Approximately 800,000 inquiries were made to local offices. There is no reason to believe that these inquiries implicitly represented violation; a person who called to determine the rules was as likely to register a complaint if the facts seemed to warrant this action.

The distribution of complaints over time did not show major fluctuations. Once the basic policies were formulated and made public, the number of alleged violations ranged between 3,000 and 5,000 per week. The weekly average for the duration of the freeze was approximately 3,500.

8. The Gallup Poll for August 29, 1971, reported that 73 percent of the respondents in a national sample supported the freeze, 17 percent were opposed, and 10 percent had no opinion. George H. Gallup, *The Gallup Poll: Public Opinion, 1935–1971* (Random House, 1972), III, 2321–22. The Harris Poll also showed a response of 73 percent in support of the freeze. *New York Times,* September 8, 1971.

9. Office of Emergency Preparedness, "Weekly Summary Report, November 3, 1971, through Close of Business, November 9, 1971" (November 13, 1971; processed), p. 2.

There was an upsurge in the middle of October immediately following the announcement of plans for Phase II, and the level of complaints remained somewhat above the average level until the end of the freeze.

The complaints received were widely dispersed among regions. Table 3 shows, however, that on the basis of population there was a somewhat disproportionate share of price and rent complaints in New England, the New York-New Jersey area, and the Western states. There is no general explanation for this distribution. In New York City, specifically, rent controls had recently been abolished after 30 years, and landlords were in the process of raising rental charges when the freeze was instituted. Thus a heavy incidence of complaints could be expected. Various watchdog groups were also particularly active in the East, and the media there gave great prominence to the rules promulgated by the Cost of Living Council.

Most of the 46,000 complaints concerned prices. Specifically, 75 per-

Table 3. *Regional Distribution of Alleged Price and Rent Violations, August 15–November 9, 1971*

OEP regions[a]	Total alleged violations	Prices		Rent	
		Alleged violations per million people	Deviation from U.S. average	Alleged violations per million people	Deviation from U.S. average
1	4,080	230.6	+34%	79.2	+86%
2	7,409	222.0	+29	61.3	+44
3	4,251	138.6	−19	35.2	−17
4	4,520	111.0	−35	22.3	−48
5	7,485	129.7	−25	30.2	−29
6	5,025	206.2	+20	30.9	−27
7	2,551	184.6	+ 7	28.6	−33
8	1,789	209.2	+22	74.4	+75
9	7,017	215.6	+25	66.7	+57
10	2,260	260.4	+51	62.7	+47
U.S. average		172.0		42.6	

Source: Office of Emergency Preparedness, "Weekly Summary Report, November 3, 1971, through Close of Business, November 9, 1971" (November 13, 1971; processed), pp. 20, 22, 23.

a. OEP regions during the freeze:
  1. Connecticut, Massachusetts, Rhode Island, Vermont, New Hampshire, Maine
  2. New York, New Jersey
  3. Pennsylvania, Maryland, West Virginia, Virginia, Delaware, District of Columbia
  4. Kentucky, Tennessee, North Carolina, South Carolina, Georgia, Florida, Mississippi, Alabama
  5. Ohio, Indiana, Illinois, Michigan, Wisconsin, Minnesota
  6. Louisiana, Arkansas, Texas, Oklahoma, New Mexico
  7. Iowa, Missouri, Kansas, Nebraska
  8. North Dakota, South Dakota, Colorado, Utah, Wyoming, Montana
  9. Arizona, California, Nevada, Hawaii
  10. Oregon, Idaho, Washington, Alaska

cent of the alleged violations involved prices, 19 percent involved rents, and only 6 percent related to wages. Because of the number of transactions involved and the continuous nature of the pricing process, it is not surprising that the large majority of the alleged violations involved prices. Rents generally are governed by fixed-term leases, and employer incentives to limit costs probably insured a low volume of wage violations.

Midway through the freeze, data were collected permitting a more refined analysis of approximately 26,000 complaints. Of these complaints, 51 percent were directed at retail establishments. As shown in Table 4, the only other sectors with a high incidence of complaints were services and insurance, with 7.6 percent and 6.9 percent of the total, respectively. The remainder was distributed widely among various industries. The significant number of complaints concerning insurance premiums was consistent with the behavior of this component of the consumer index and, as noted above, probably reflected a lack of understanding of the appropriate regulations. The flurry of complaints involving services, on the other hand, clearly arose from the difficulty of defining established price-quality relationships and from the lack of prior, explicit price information.

The reported violations in the retail sector were about equally divided between chain stores and single-unit establishments. Of the complaints lodged against retail establishments, the dominant product category was

Table 4. *Alleged Price Violations within Industry Classifications*

Classification	Alleged violations	Percentage of total
Real estate	653	2.5
Construction	56	*
Manufacturing	432	1.6
Retail trade	13,364	50.6
Wholesale trade	936	3.5
Services and repairs	2,014	7.6
Utilities	831	3.1
Government	584	2.2
Insurance	1,806	6.8
Importer	42	*
Mining	6	*
Other	3,218	12.2
Not available	2,493	9.4
Total	26,435	100.0

Source: OEP, "Summary Report through Close of Business," p. B-3 Percentages rounded.
* Less than 0.05 percent.

food, which involved 45 percent of the alleged violations. Automotive services was a distant second with 5 percent of the complaints. The preponderance of complaints over food prices undoubtedly mirrored the consumer's day-to-day sensitivity to these prices and the complications posed by the fact that so-called raw agricultural products were exempt from the freeze while processed food products were covered.

The problems of comprehension and enforcement were also formidable in automotive services. In this case, many gas stations had raised their prices from the discount levels that prevailed immediately before the freeze. The higher prices were permissible in most instances because a "substantial volume of transactions" had taken place at these levels sometime during the base period.

Individuals speaking for themselves alone made the overwhelming proportion of the complaints—approximately 80 percent. Only 10 percent of the alleged violations were reported by businesses, and, surprisingly, less than 1 percent were brought to the attention of the IRS by labor unions. Although labor unions in several locales had complained vociferously of widespread noncompliance, few of these complaints apparently were filed with the IRS. Over 50 percent of the total complaints involved business units in the city, as contrasted to the suburbs and rural areas.

The record of alleged rent violations reveals no glaring deficiency in the enforcement procedures for this area. Those complaints for which there was full information were evenly divided between small structures, with one to four rental units, and those with five units or more. Almost all the citations involved rent increases, while only 3 percent related to alleged reductions in services. The low incidence of complaints that services had been trimmed could be expected in view of the short duration of the freeze. Approximately 95 percent of the complaints involved residential as contrasted to commerical units; and 76 percent of the reported residential violations occurred in the central city.

Consistent with the performance of the index of average hourly earnings, there were few complaints of wage violations, and these showed no distinctive pattern. Although the data are incomplete, there is some evidence that wage regulations were breached more frequently by non-union employers than by unionized employers.[10] This difference is consistent with

10. Of the 1,745 complaints of wage violations filed during the freeze, data are available concerning the union or non-union status of the firm involved for 797 complaints. Of this total, 552 involved non-union workers, and 245 involved union workers. *Ibid.*

the fact that non-union employers are not restrained by periodic collective bargaining agreements and may initiate wage increases on an individual and continuous basis. Table 5 reveals that the industrial distribution of wage complaints extended to all sectors. The greatest number of citations, however, were made against governmental employers. Wage increases for public employees were highly visible, and the controversies with the state of Texas and teacher organizations probably focused attention on such developments.

The disposition of the complaints, as reported by OEP and IRS, supports the judgment that the enforcement program was generally effective and that much of this effectiveness could be attributed to voluntary compliance. Of the 46,000 complaints received by IRS, approximately 62 percent were found to be without merit after a more precise determination of the facts. All except a small fraction of the remaining complaints were satisfactorily resolved after informal discussions with IRS personnel. For example, a complaint concerning an increase in the price of gasoline would be dismissed when it was shown that the vendor had had a "substantial volume of transactions" at the higher price during the base period. Approximately 200 alleged violations were referred to OEP regional offices for review, and only 73 were ultimately forwarded to the national office. A tiny proportion of the total complaints—about 37—went to the Depart-

Table 5. *Alleged Wage Violations within Industry Classifications*

Classification	Alleged violations	Percentage of total
Real estate	33	1.9
Construction	57	3.3
Manufacturing	200	11.5
Retail trade	116	6.6
Wholesale trade	30	1.7
Services and repairs	73	4.2
Utilities	29	1.7
Government	342	19.6
Insurance	38	2.2
Importer	1	*
Mining	0	*
Other	514	29.5
Not available	312	17.9
Total	1,745	100.0

Source: OEP, "Summary Report through Close of Business," p. B-12. Percentages rounded.
* Less than 0.05 percent.

ment of Justice for action.[11] Many of these unresolved cases involved either season tickets for sporting events or teachers' salaries.

The record of compliance was further confirmed by the results of independent monitoring. Beginning in the second month of the freeze, the enforcement program was expanded to include active monitoring of business firms by IRS field personnel. These compliance checks were carried out by IRS agents in the course of their normal activities associated with the administration of the tax laws and, in some cases, on a special basis. Doubtless the quality and intensity of these inspections were highly variable. Nonetheless, the results revealed a picture of broad compliance. From the end of September until the termination of the freeze in mid-November, IRS initiated over 85,000 compliance checks. In 92 percent of the cases no violations were found. Where there were violations, immediate compliance was forthcoming in over half of the cases. A significant proportion of the unresolved violations concerned the posting of price lists—a requirement that was subject to frequent change and clarification.

At the administrative level then, the record indicates that the stabilization program was not beset by widespread noncompliance. Many of the complaints probably arose from incomplete understanding of the rules governing the freeze or confusion in their applicability. Where bona fide infractions were identified, voluntary compliance was forthcoming in most instances. If a dominant problem could be identified, it probably was food prices in retail establishments. Even in this case, it is not clear what proportion of the reported violations reflected the misapplication of existing rules as contrasted to efforts at willful evasion. In general, the risk incurred in initiating a comprehensive freeze with only a skeletal enforcement staff and relying primarily on voluntary compliance appeared to have been vindicated.

Problems of Enforcement

The positive record of compliance was achieved despite the persistence of acute problems in the implementation of the enforcement program. These problems involved administrative incapacities, overt resistance, and inherent difficulties in fashioning an appropriate remedy.

11. Since some cases were resolved after referral to the Justice Department, the total number actually forwarded was somewhat greater than 37.

Few cases of noncompliance resulted in court action by the government. This experience to some extent reflected the high degree of voluntary compliance and the willingness of alleged violators to mend their ways; but it also was the product of enduring bureaucratic deficiencies. First, the procedures for systematically investigating complaints, compiling the necessary evidence for OEP and Justice Department review, and deciding what action to take never functioned smoothly. As the stabilization program was organized, the sequence of steps for investigating and combating violations involved four different agencies—IRS, OEP, the Civil Division of the Justice Department, and the Cost of Living Council. Under ordinary circumstances, the problems of coordination would have been severe; with each agency in the process of developing its own operational guides under extreme time pressure, stable and effective coordination was virtually impossible to achieve.

IRS investigators had to be instructed in the techniques and scope of their investigations to build a creditable case. OEP officials at the regional level had to work with Assistant U.S. Attorneys who were often assigned to the program with scant notice and little background. In many instances, individual cases moved from the field to national headquarters and back to the field in several cycles before there was an adequate basis for determining whether legal action was advisable. Usually when an alleged infraction was pressed in court, the particular case had to be tracked on a daily basis through the system until the necessary information had been collected and the appropriate documents prepared. The Director of OEP, the Assistant Attorney-General in charge of the Civil Division, and the Executive Director of the Cost of Living Council had to meet on a regular basis to insure that the system gave forth some output.

Second, the Civil Division of the Justice Department, which was responsible for conducting all litigation on behalf of the government, held the usual professional bias of trial lawyers. As an operating convention, the Civil Division did not feel that a case should be brought to litigation unless a clear principle of law was involved and there was a high probability of success. This philosophy was a constructive guide in discharging the normal responsibilities of the division; however, it clashed with the overall enforcement strategy developed for the freeze, which placed great emphasis on building public confidence by providing dramatic examples of enforcement.

Because of the administrative difficulties and differences in approach, the question of litigation was considered continuously by the top officials concerned. No case was taken to court unless there was agreement by all agencies. This process was extremely laborious and worked against the initiation of a large number of court cases. Compromises were inevitably made so that the complaints that were prosecuted reflected both the interests of the litigators and the Cost of Living Council. For example, a rent violator was brought into court because it was a highly visible enforcement action that would benefit directly the ordinary citizen. At the same time the case provided an opportunity to test the "unit-by-unit rule" that was applicable to rent ceilings.

The difficulty of obtaining compliance was compounded when there was a general unwillingness to accept the regulations governing the freeze and the aggrieved party adopted an adversary position. This was the case in dealings with the school bus operators. Contracts to provide school bus services at increased rates generally had been negotiated between school districts and the various bus companies before the freeze was initiated. Because the service had not actually been delivered at the higher price, however, the increases were not allowed. At the same time, many of the bus companies alleged that they had raised the salaries of the bus drivers and other personnel on the assumption that revenues would be increased. According to representatives of an association of school bus operators, about 350 companies were caught in this squeeze. Nonetheless, the Cost of Living Council ruled that the higher bus rates were not allowable and that the additional costs would have to be absorbed for the period of the freeze.

Faced with this circumstance, several bus operators declared that they would refuse to provide transportation services—which would not be a violation of the Economic Stabilization Act. The most important case involved the New York City school system, where there had been an increase of more than 20 percent in rates and the bus company stated that it could not operate at the old price. After prolonged discussion, IRS sent a special team of investigators to assess the cost justification for the price increase. The IRS team reported that the company's cost estimates were excessive and that it could continue to provide services without creating a "gross inequity." Following this report, the company retreated from its position and did agree to provide transportation for school children throughout the freeze.

Less success was registered in dealing with the problem of teachers' salaries. The fact that the timing of the freeze coincided with the beginning of a new school year meant that the determination of rules governing teachers' salary increases had to be handed down hurriedly and without a full appreciation of the variety that existed in teacher compensation practices in the 17,000 school districts around the country. The first statements of policy were complex and ambiguous and resulted in conflicting interpretations in the field.

When widespread noncompliance was discovered, the Cost of Living Council staff attempted to tighten the rules. By this time, the major teacher organizations, the National Education Association and the American Federation of Teachers, had adopted a general stance of resistance and were exploiting any existing confusion. State educational administrators also pressed aggressively for the full implementation of scheduled salary increases. Eventually, the regulations covering salary increases for teachers were clarified; however, this step did little to improve the situation. The two court cases that were initiated by the government appeared to have little effect. Although the extent of noncompliance with respect to teachers' salaries was never known, one survey taken by OEP midway in the freeze indicated that as many as 1,000 school districts were probably out of compliance with the rules.

The experience with the teacher organizations during the freeze contrasted notably with the reaction of organized labor in general. A series of broadsides attacking the inequity of the stabilization program notwithstanding, both the AFL-CIO and individual unions responded with restraint and uncertainty to the new circumstances. Because the AFL-CIO had called for wage and price controls only a few days before August 15, it was politically difficult to oppose the program directly. For the greater part, organized labor maintained a passive hostility toward the stabilization program and made little effort to influence its administration. Instead, several unions initiated court suits challenging various aspects of the program. The most contentious issue involved the status of deferred increases that were scheduled for the freeze period. The denial of the deferred increases engendered a bitter response after the freeze was over. The issue was finally resolved to organized labor's advantage by Congressional action in December 1971 when the Economic Stabilization Act was amended to provide for retroactive pay in most situations.

No cases were reported in which a strike was initiated to force an employer to violate the freeze. Indeed, as shown in Table 6, the number of strikes reported in the period from August to November of 1971 was significantly less than the 1966–70 average for the same four months of the year. This record was distinguished from the trend during the first seven months of 1971, when the incidence of strikes was a little above the five-year average.

Table 6. *Work Stoppages per Month, 1971 and 1966–70*

| Month | Number of stoppages | | Ratio, 1971 to 1966–70 average |
	1971	1966–70 average	
January	416	292	1.42
February	359	323	1.11
March	457	390	1.17
April	550	518	1.06
May	612	611	1.00
June	617	539	1.14
July	499	494	1.01
August	438	473	0.93
September	352	480	0.73
October	304	454	0.67
November	315	328	0.96
December	219	192	1.14

Sources: U.S. Bureau of Labor Statistics, "Work Stoppages: October 1972," USDL 72-808 (November 29, 1972; processed), p. 2; BLS, *Analysis of Work Stoppages, 1970*, Bulletin 1727 (1972), pp. 55–58.

When confronted by the freeze, many individual unions appeared to adopt a wait-and-see approach rather than engaging in disruptive tactics. According to information furnished by the BLS, 156 contracts covering 1,000 or more employees expired between September 1 and November 14, 1971. Some 63 of these, or 40 percent of the contracts, had not been re-negotiated by the end of the freeze.[12] It is not unusual for collective bargaining agreements to be extended beyond their expiration dates on a day-to-day basis, but the fact that so large a percentage of pending negotiations were postponed indicates that the parties were awaiting the formulation of the post-freeze wage standard before they committed themselves to a new contract. The tacit acceptance of the freeze by organized labor was an important ingredient in the compliance program. Experience abroad indicates that without such acceptance an economic stabilization program is not likely to endure.

The effectiveness of the enforcement program was also diluted when adequate remedies were not available to deal with violations. This was the circumstance in seeking compliance with the rules governing stock options. Under the regulations promulgated by the Cost of Living Council, an employee could not exercise stock options during the freeze unless the option was scheduled to expire within that period. Although several instances

12. Compiled by the author from data provided by the BLS.

were identified in which stock options had been illegally exercised, a suitable remedy was not readily available. One course of action considered was to force the person who had exercised the stock option to sell the stock on the open market and divide the proceeds between the company and the employee in the same proportion in which they shared the purchase price. This alternative was rejected on the grounds that it would encounter severe legal difficulties and would elicit countersuits by the respondents. As a result, the violations were quietly ignored. This inaction was rationalized through the contention that the violations were *de minimis* and would have no inflationary effect. Nonetheless, the residual inequity was serious even though it did not capture public attention.

The availability of remedies was constrained in some cases by the short time span of the freeze. Several situations came to light in which contracts were negotiated during the freeze for the purchase of goods at a time beyond the termination date of the freeze at prices higher than the allowable ceiling. Many of these long-term contracts involved heavy capital equipment which was produced on a custom basis. Similarly, collective bargaining agreements were negotiated with effective dates after the expiration of the freeze. Legally and practically, there was little that CLC could do in these cases since it was not clear what its authority would be after November 14, 1971. CLC had to be content with a limp statement that all parties who entered into such long-term contracts did so at their own peril and that these transactions would be subject to the rules that were applicable during the post-freeze program.

One potential problem of enforcement is noteworthy because it did not occur. Any program as far-ranging as the wage-price freeze of 1971 might be expected to engender political pressures to modify or soften the application of the rules in particular cases. Surprisingly, very few such pressures were manifested during the freeze. Some requests were made by individual Congressmen to "understand the unique circumstances" in specific cases; however, these petitions were usually *pro forma* and invariably were rejected after staff analysis. No instance came to light during the freeze in which enforcement action, or inaction, was dictated by purely political considerations.[13] The apolitical nature of the enforcement program was abetted by the fact that Congress was out of session until the second week of

13. The one case in which political considerations were important involved the sugar refining industry. However, the decision to permit an increase in the price of raw sugar could be considered equitable and had no effect upon the price of refined sugar paid by the consumer. See pp. 78–80.

September and was not available as a ready conduit for special interests. In addition, the widespread public acceptance of the freeze diminished the temptation for particular Congressmen or operatives in the executive branch to intervene for narrow political reasons. Most important, top officials of CLC provided the necessary support to insulate the staff from the need to accommodate external pressures.

The one case that raised the greatest political sensitivities involved the military pay bill. The administration had been pressing for a large increase in military pay as part of its program to phase out the draft and to build an all-volunteer army. These efforts came to fruition in September when an increase in military pay was included in legislation amending the Military Selective Service Act of 1967.[14] The question was then whether the pay increase should become effective immediately or should be deferred to the end of the freeze. The issue went to the President, who concurred in CLC's recommendation that the increase should be postponed until the beginning of Phase II.

Litigation and Court Action

As indicated above, actual litigation was used primarily as a defensive tactic and as a technique for public relations to demonstrate the government's determination to enforce the program in a vigorous manner. During the freeze, the government was a party in 45 cases. In 8 of these cases, the suits were filed directly by the Justice Department against an alleged violator. In 37 cases, the government was itself sued.

The scoreboard of judicial action indicated that the tactical objectives of legal proceedings generally were achieved. Of the cases filed by the Justice Department, the government won three and lost one, and the others had not been decided by the end of the freeze. Of the cases involving the United States as defendant, the government won three and lost none. The rest of the cases were still pending when Phase II began. More important, the cases that were decided with some degree of judicial credence dealt with questions that were crucial to the stabilization program. The final disposition of the other suits was not critical to the effectiveness of the program, and indeed, because of the risk of adverse decisions, some delay was desirable until the basic enabling legislation could be amended.

14. P.L. 92-129 (September 28, 1971).

The most important case adjudicated during the freeze posed a constitutional test to the economic stabilization program. In a suit filed in the federal district court in Washington, D.C., the Amalgamated Meat Cutters and Butcher Workmen of North America, AFL-CIO, attacked the constitutionality of the Economic Stabilization Act and sought to set aside a CLC ruling which blocked the major meat packing companies from granting on September 6, 1971, a wage increase that had been negotiated in a 1970 collective bargaining agreement.

In its suit, the union attacked the program in the broadest possible terms. It alleged that the Stabilization Act was an unconstitutional delegation of legislative power to the Executive branch, that the statute failed to provide adequate standards and safeguards, and that the procedures established by the President and CLC denied due process under the Administrative Procedure Act. If the union's claims had been sustained, the entire program would have been overturned and rendered inoperative.

In view of the important questions involved, a special three-judge panel of the district court was convened in Washington. Acting with speed, the court upheld the constitutionality of the Economic Stabilization Act and the actions taken by the President and CLC to implement the intent of Congress. In its decision, the court relied heavily on the legislative history of the statute and previous experience with economic controls during World War II and the Korean War. The judicial panel also ruled that adequate safeguards were included in the statute and that further protection against capricious administrative action was provided by the opportunity to obtain judicial review. In focusing on the main issue raised by the Meat Cutters' case, Judge Harold Leventhal stated:

The legislative power granted to Congress by the Constitution includes the power to avail itself of "the necessary resources of flexibility and practicality— to perform its function." The spaciousness of the legislative authority is underscored by the following quotations from the *Yakus* opinion voicing the elements of the applicable principles: "The Constitution as a continuously operative charter of the government does not demand the impossible or the impractical." Congress is free to delegate legislative authority provided it has exercised "the essentials of the legislative function" of determining the basic legislative policy and formulating a rule of conduct held satisfied by "the rule, with penal sanctions, that prices shall not be greater than those fixed by maximum price regulations which conform to standards and will tend to further the policy which Congress has established." The key question is not answered by noting that the authority delegated is broad, or broader than Congress might have selected if it had chosen to operate within a narrower range. The issue is whether the legislative description of the task assigned "sufficiently marks the field within which the Administrator is to act so that it may be known whether he has kept within it in compliance with the legislative will."[15]

The court answered this question in the affirmative. When the decision was handed down, the Meat Cutters sought a direct appeal to the Supreme Court—a procedure which is permissible in such cases. But the fact that Supreme Court consideration was far off meant that the constitutional foundation of the stabilization program would remain intact during the freeze. In addition, the fact that the administration was seeking amendments to the Economic Stabilization Act to remedy the more glaring defects in the statute made it likely that the case would be moot by the time the freeze had ended.

The other major legal issue treated by the courts during the freeze involved the basic regulation applicable to rental units. Here, CLC had imposed a unit-by-unit rule which modified the concept of "substantial transactions" used for other prices. In two cases, one in Texas and one in Ohio, landlords had clearly violated the unit-by-unit rule. The facts were not at issue, but the landlords alleged that the application of this rule to rental units alone was arbitrary and capricious and inconsistent with the executive order implementing the Economic Stabilization Act. In both cases, the federal courts sustained the government and rejected the contention that the differences between the regulations applicable to rental units and those applied to other goods and services were arbitrary.[16] The Texas decision, which came during the freeze, was extremely significant in preserving the legal integrity of the stabilization program. In addition, these two cases established a powerful precedent that could be applied in other cases where modifications of general standards had been made.

The results of the litigation involving teachers was less comforting. In one key case, the government sued the school board of Jefferson Parish in New Orleans to enjoin it from paying teachers salary increases that were scheduled to become effective during the freeze. The district court rejected the government's petition and cited inconsistencies in the regulations that covered this issue. Moreover, the court noted that the salary increase had

15. *Amalgamated Meat Cutters and Butcher Workmen of North America, AFL-CIO v. Connally,* 337 F. Supp. 737 (D.D.C. 1971). It is interesting to note that Judge Leventhal had been Assistant General Counsel for the Office of Price Administration during World War II.

16. *United States* v. *Lieb,* 333 F. Supp. 424 (W.D. Tex. 1971); affirmed 462 F. 2d 1161 (TECA, No. 5-1, 1972). *United States* v. *Huber Investment Corporation,* 337 F. Supp. 507 (S.D. Ohio 1972).

been initiated pursuant to a state law that had been passed during the 1968 legislative session.[17]

Although the government had won favorable decisions in teacher cases in a few state courts and in a federal suit heard in California, the Jefferson Parish decision was potentially highly damaging. As a result, it was decided to delay any appeal to the circuit court. Through this tactic, the Jefferson Parish decision would remain merely one of many decisions at the district court level and would not have persuasive effect in other courts as would be the case if an adverse decision were handed down by a court of appeals.[18]

The Justice Department attorneys also were apprehensive over the various sports cases. Even though the Civil Division's lawyers believed that the government's position was reinforced by rent cases, they questioned whether the court would sustain the ruling that the price of season tickets, set long before the freeze, could be rolled back. The test cases in this area dragged on far beyond the termination of the freeze.

As an epilogue to the freeze, the Temporary Emergency Court of Appeals, a special federal court set up to handle cases during Phase II of the stabilization program, sustained CLC in its ruling which rolled back football ticket prices at the University of Southern California. As in the Atlanta Falcons case, the university had raised the price of football tickets well before the freeze commenced, but the games did not take place until after August 15. The university balked at OEP's order to roll back prices and to refund the extra charge and sought declaratory judgment in federal district court. The lower court sustained the university and ruled that CLC had exceeded its authority by applying its rules retroactively and ordering refunds. The Temporary Emergency Court of Appeals overturned the decision and, in a sweeping opinion, stated that CLC had acted properly under its wide grant of authority from the President. Of particular importance was the fact that TECA affirmed the "delivered service" concept used in defining a "transaction" for purposes of the stabilization program.[19]

Although most of the court cases instituted by the government were de-

17. *United States* v. *Jefferson Parish School Board,* 333 F. Supp. 418 (E.D. La. 1971).

18. The district court decision in the Jefferson Parish case was not appealed by the government. Congressional action permitting retroactive wage increases essentially made the case moot.

19. *University of Southern California* v. *Cost of Living Council,* 342 F. Supp. 606 (C.D. Calif. 1972); overturned TECA, No. 9-1, 1972.

fensive in nature, the Cost of Living Council did take one venturesome legal initiative at the end of the freeze. The Cincinnati Transit corporation had been authorized by the city's Public Utilities Director to reduce bus service to offset the firm's operating losses. The reduction in service was in lieu of a fare increase pending efforts to relieve the financial squeeze on the system through a Metropolitan Transit Authority. OEP investigated the matter in response to complaints and concluded that the reduction in service constituted a price increase and violated the freeze. Under CLC rules, a reduction in service was permissible to adjust to changing demand but not to maintain a rate of return on investment, i.e., to cut operating losses.

The government filed suit to force the firm to restore the previous level of service. The question of an appropriate remedy was complicated by the fact that Cincinnati Transit also instituted a fare increase at the beginning of Phase II, leading to another suit, this one filed by the Price Commission. However, in enjoining the company from making further service cuts or price increases the federal district court did sustain OEP's original finding that a violation of the freeze had been committed.[20]

The administrative record of compliance generally showed salutary results. At the outset of the freeze, the President stated his desire to avoid a "huge bureaucracy" and his intention to rely heavily on voluntary compliance. Ironically, as the program developed, what appeared to be a discretionary policy was an accommodation to the only real course that was open to the administration. In view of the short duration of the freeze, the ad hoc nature of many of the regulations, and the limitations of resources and legislative authority, effective compliance could be attained only through voluntary compliance. Whether the apparent compliance was a consequence of the strategy that had been adopted or whether it would have taken place anyway, the enforcement effort did provide the necessary mantle of federal authority without creating either disincentives for compliance or widespread resentment that would undermine efforts to achieve the stabilization goals.

20. *United States* v. *Cincinnati Transit, Inc.*, 337 F. Supp. 1068 (S.D. Ohio 1972).

IX

Lessons and Limitations

At the end of the prescribed 90 days, the wage-price freeze ran its course and was supplanted by the more complex system of controls designated as Phase II. In the fanfare generated by the onset of Phase II, the freeze was submerged in the overall stabilization program to such an extent that its strengths and shortcomings became indistinct. Because the wage-price freeze of 1971 represented American loss of innocence in the use of peacetime controls, it is useful to review the lessons of this experience. Reaction to future temptation will be determined by whether the episode is remembered with pain or pleasure. In this respect, the insights provided by the 1971 experience fall into two categories: those that relate to the operational aspects of a wage-price freeze and those that shed some light on the utility of a freeze as a component of incomes policy in general.

Making a Freeze Effective

There is little doubt that a comprehensive freeze can restrain wage and price increases effectively in the short run. To be sure, the success of the freeze of 1971 was facilitated by the fact that it was imposed on a cool economy marked by considerable slack in the labor force and industrial capacity. Nevertheless, to the extent that there is broad public support for an activist government policy, it seems likely that a freeze can brake temporarily the upward movement of wages and prices even when the economy is working at or near full capacity. Overall, the freeze worked with a high degree of effectiveness, was remarkably free from political influences in its execution, and demonstrated that the governmental apparatus can be adequate to the task with minimal preparation. Moreover, the freeze was carried out without attempting to "manage" the economy in any systematic way. To be sure, there was a sensitivity to questions of resource allocation and adequacy of supply; but during the relatively short time the freeze lasted, it was possible to administer the program by simple rules that gave greater weight to equity and comprehension than to marginal adjustments in efficiency.

The record of the 90-day period also indicates that a freeze will probably exercise greater short-term restraint on wages than on prices. This differential impact appears to result from several factors. First, as a technical matter, it is much easier to control wages than prices. Pricing practices generally are more varied and complex than methods of compensation, and the task of merely identifying a price increase often requires considerable analysis and expertise.

Second, price changes usually take place on a continuous basis and may involve differential increases for thousands of individual commodities, while wage changes are often made on a fixed cycle of across-the-board adjustments. Hence wage increases are more visible and amenable to control.

Third, there is an asymmetry in the employer's incentives for limiting wage increases on the one hand and raising prices on the other. An employer will almost always have an incentive to reduce costs by checking wage increases, especially when other employers are under similar restraints and are unlikely to bid away his labor force. On the price side, however, the employer still has the usual incentives to maximize revenues through price increases when the nature of demand makes this action appropriate. Certainly, the paucity of complaints of wage increases and the behavior of the wage indexes during the 1971 freeze indicated that few employers felt any compulsion to evade the wage controls.

The events of 1971 also suggest that the effectiveness of a wage-price freeze will be enhanced when it is implemented with little or no warning. Any extended talks probably will result in anticipatory increases in wages and prices by those parties who seek to exploit immediate economic advantages or who believe that a freeze will otherwise penalize them unfairly. Any prolonged discussion of the rules of the game inevitably will provide a forum for the airing of grievances, real or imagined.

Conversely, the advantages of surprise may be diminished by political costs, since the sudden initiation of a freeze curtails the opportunity for consultation with major economic interest groups in the economy. Even though the AFL-CIO Executive Council had endorsed controls five days before the freeze was ordered, the reaction of the labor federation was rancorous at best.[1] This initial response colored the AFL-CIO's subsequent participation in the economic stabilization program. Even though the cries

---

1. "Statements Adopted by the AFL-CIO Executive Council, August 9–10, 1971" (American Federation of Labor and Congress of Industrial Organizations, 1971; processed), p. 4.

of outrage were inspired, in part, by political considerations, organized labor's hostility probably could have been dampened if some prior notice had been given. For political decision makers, the problem is one of balancing the immediate tactical gains from surprise against the longer-term costs resulting from the erosion of the consensus that is necessary to support a comprehensive system of control. In the summer of 1971 there was considerable evidence that a broad consensus for controls did exist; therefore, the political costs of imposing the freeze without wide prior consultation were not weighed as heavily as they might be in other circumstances.

The need for surprise should not preclude some planning for the implementation of a wage-price freeze. It is true that the administration's shift in economic policy was initiated with an urgency that did not permit extensive planning of policies and procedures. The basic decisions were made by the top officials of government—including the President—in a 48-hour period. In addition, earlier administration statements opposing any form of economic controls did not provide constructive cues to encourage planning at lower, bureaucratic levels. The total government commitment to planning an economic stabilization program at the time of the freeze was one middle-level civil servant in OEP. Also, such planning as had taken place had a wartime flavor and was concerned primarily with strategic materials rather than the rules that would govern the operation of a peacetime economy.

Despite the unique circumstances surrounding the wage-price freeze of 1971, one of the consequences of this episode was to add formal incomes policies to the repertoire of economic precedents that political leaders can draw upon in the future. It is not conducive to intelligent policy formulation and administration to conduct a program of such magnitude under conditions of acute improvisation. Once the freeze was initiated, maximum support was provided, and the machinery of government operated with a high degree of efficiency. But the navigator should not be drafting the charts while the ship is moving through the water. At the least, planning can help to avoid errors in judgment that result inevitably from the need to make ad hoc decisions under extreme time pressure. Because of the absence of foresight, significant conceptual or tactical errors were made concerning college tuition and teachers' salaries—the most controversial and least satisfactorily handled issues during the freeze.

Ongoing responsibility for planning incomes policies should lie with some high-level agency, preferably the Council of Economic Advisers. The little advance planning that was carried out before the freeze was executed by the Office of Management and Budget. Although this agency has a high degree of versatility and professionalism, it does not have the special competence to draft possible operating policies and procedures. CEA, on the other hand, has general responsibilities for the performance of the economy and can enlist the resources of other agencies for detailed staff work.

It is impossible, of course, to anticipate all the problems that will have to be confronted during a period of price control. In any case, the helmsmen will require considerable discretion and dexterity. Some shoals can be avoided, however, if prior attention is given to basic policy issues. The coverage of the freeze should be adapted to the current analysis of the causes of inflation and the policy objectives of the stabilization program. Standards should be developed that distinguish between those future commitments, entered into before the freeze, which should be barred because they would undermine the efficacy of the program and those which should be permitted to take effect for reasons of equity or efficiency.

A careful review should be conducted of government price support programs, particularly those in the agricultural sector, that are inconsistent with the goals of a freeze, and authority may be sought to modify these programs when controls are imposed. The distinctions between taxes, fees, and licenses as charges for local government services should be delineated so that the treatment of these "prices" will not be arbitrary. The various forms of compensation should be analyzed in detail to identify those components that reflect productivity increases or the cashing-in of prior compensation which falls due as contrasted to those that impose net increments to labor cost. And a sophisticated effort should be made to enumerate the circumstances under which cost pass-throughs may be permitted to relieve severe inequities or threats to the stability of supply of important commodities.

The planning function should also encompass the array of incomes policies and not the alternatives concerning a wage-price freeze alone. A wage-price freeze is not and cannot be a self-contained instrument of incomes policy. It is only an interim step that must be linked to more complex measures. Moreover, a sensible choice of policies during a freeze depends upon the nature and objectives of the post-freeze program. For example, prior knowledge of Phase II probably would have affected the early decisions relating to deferred increases and other forward commitments. At the same time, the lack of guidance concerning the post-freeze program meant that the freeze of 1971 was administered within its own frame of reference, and several decisions were made that limited the government's discretion in formulating plans for Phase II.

Lack of adequate planning contributed to a major shortcoming in the administration of the freeze. That is, as the freeze progressed, it became clear that the coverage was too extensive for economic and administrative purposes. As noted above, the justification for virtually universal coverage was twofold. First, sensitivity about equity was a powerful consideration pushing in the direction of comprehensive coverage. Severe political consequences were foreseen if some sectors of the economy were covered by the freeze while others were exempted. Second, the almost universal coverage of the freeze was designed to have a dramatic impact on expectations. Presumably the President's intent to deal with inflation would be more forcefully revealed to the extent that the freeze was comprehensive in scope.

This rationale for the inclusive coverage of the freeze was probably overstated. It is questionable whether the inclusion of military pay, objects of art, used cars, stamps, and related commodities significantly affected the public's sense of equity or its assessment of the administration's will in coping with inflation. Indeed, the one major exclusion from the freeze—raw agricultural products—could be presumed to have a more profound impact on equity and the public's expectations than the exemption of any other sector of the economy. Nonetheless, this exclusion was made from the outset, and the problems that were created were not insuperable or even severe. The failure to refine the coverage of the freeze meant that an inordinate amount of scarce administrative resources had to be diverted to looking into peripheral economic activities which had little significance for the objectives of the stabilization program.

An overly rigorous approach was also taken to some of the other basic policies governing the freeze. In broad terms, the Cost of Living Council had a choice between a "hard" freeze and a "soft" freeze. At the outset, it was recognized that some adjustments would have to take place because of economic or equity requirements. In addition, it was desirable to minimize the pressures that would have to be vented when the freeze was terminated. The preferred strategy was to "talk tough but walk softly." This concept proved to be troublesome in practice. Public acceptance of the freeze, the fact that basic policies were not on hand to check zealous officials, and the struggle for consistency all combined to produce highly restrictive policies.

Overall, the public's tolerance for these stringent policies proved to be greater than expected, and the freeze "worked" within its short period of reference. On the other hand, this unremitting "toughness" clearly contributed to the magnitude of the post-freeze "bubble" that distorted wage and price movements in the first few months of Phase II and made it extremely difficult to maintain the credibility of the stabilization program.[2] In addition, certain inequities that arose were difficult to justify even on the theory of random occurrence that was used to justify decisions in individual cases. The policy toward wage increases that were retroactive to a date prior to the freeze perhaps best exemplified the unfortunate consequences of the jesuitical approach to policy formulation.

Hindsight reveals that some relaxation of the transaction rule would have been desirable, especially as applied to commitments made before the freeze was imposed. With greater flexibility, the problems with the teachers, bond issues, commodity markets, and tuition would have been minimized. In addition, the transition to Phase II could have been eased by reducing both labor's sense of repression because of the denial of deferred wage increases and the sharp upsurge in wages that took place in December 1971. As the situation developed, Congress permitted retroactivity for wage increases denied during the freeze.[3] As a result, that limited segment of the

2. In the period November 1971–February 1972 the consumer price index rose at an annual rate of 4.8 percent, the wholesale price index by 6.9 percent, and the index of hourly earnings for private non-farm production workers (adjusted for inter-industry shifts and overtime in manufacturing only) by 9.4 percent. *Economic Report of the President, January 1973*, pp. 57, 228.

Although these increases were expected by government officials, the magnitude of the bubble caused considerable consternation in the press and on the part of the public. For a while there was some question whether Phase II would be adequate to the task. Despite the size of the post-freeze wage and price increases, however, two analysts, using different methodological approaches, concluded that the stabilization program from August 1971 to July 1972 had prevented increases that would have taken place in the absence of controls. See Barry Bosworth, "Phase II: The U.S. Experiment with an Incomes Policy," and Robert J. Gordon, "Wage Price Controls and the Shifting Phillips Curve: How Reliable Is the Economic Evidence?" both in *Brookings Papers on Economic Activity* (2:1972), pp. 343–83 and 385–421, respectively.

3. The amendments to the Economic Stabilization Act, passed in December 1971, allowed retroactive pay increases in most situations in which some commitment had been made prior to August 15, 1971. In general, the amendments provided that back wages could be paid for any increase which would have been granted except for the freeze. Conditions were stipulated, however: namely, that any such increases must have been provided for by law, contract, agreement, or practice established prior to August 15, 1971, and that prices must have been advanced, productivity increased, taxes raised, appropriations made, or funds otherwise raised or provided for in order to cover such increases. In cases where agreements were made prior to August 15 but the other conditions were not met, back wages could be paid as long as the payments were not "unreasonably inconsistent" with the purposes of the Stabilization Act. P.L. 92-210 (December 22, 1971), sec. 203.

The amendments permitting retroactive pay were aggressively sought by the AFL-CIO and the teacher organizations. No manifest opposition was forthcoming from management spokesmen.

labor force that was covered by pre-freeze collective bargaining agreements benefited while others, in less favorable circumstances, were denied wage increases that might otherwise have taken place. Perhaps the greatest inequity arose from this ex post effort to provide "justice" to one group without affording the same relief to other claimants.

No conclusive judgment can be made concerning the optimal length of a freeze. Undoubtedly, this will vary with the degree of public support, the bureaucratic capacity for enforcement, and the underlying economic pressures. The original plan considered at Camp David specified a duration of 60 days. This period was later extended to 90 days. Whatever the optimal duration might be, under the circumstances that prevailed in mid-1971, 90 days was not excessive. It is equally clear, however, that by the end of the freeze the use of highly rigid, general policies on specific problems was creating severe strains on the dike. Probably the legal force of the freeze could have carried it for a few more months; but the administrative and intellectual processes had become entangled to such an extent that effective program management was extremely difficult to maintain.

Whatever the problems of policy formulation, the record of the freeze did indicate that controls could be administered without what President Nixon characterized as a "huge bureaucracy." Beginning with an initial involvement of 3 persons, the program reached a peak manpower complement of approximately 3,000. The entire staff was recruited from existing personnel resources within the federal government. Through a sense of urgency and dedication, and with the maximum support of the top officers of government, the staff built an effective administrative apparatus from scratch and maintained the momentum of the program. The choice of OEP and IRS proved to be especially felicitous, for both agencies performed with great energy and skill. By conventional standards of government performance, the wage-price freeze of 1971 must be rated as something of a bureaucratic miracle.

Aside from any ideological distaste for massive bureaucracies, the personnel requirements of a wage-price freeze are not inherently great. Any strategy for enforcement must rely preponderantly on voluntary compliance. The staff requirements are essentially threefold. First, there must be an ongoing capability to make policies and to apply them in individual cases. Second, there must be a widespread communications network to convey specific rules and regulations to the public. Third, there should be some personnel who police the program by independent monitoring or resolving complaints. Because a wage-price freeze usually will be short-lived, a relatively Spartan staff will suffice. Indeed, a small staff is desirable to the extent that it avoids excessively complicated procedures and tendencies toward self-perpetuation.

The sense of bureaucratic achievement should not obscure a serious deficiency in the conduct of the freeze. Private economic decisions are essentially the exercise of individual liberty supported by law. Normal government interventions into the product and labor markets are conditioned by the requirements of due process arduously developed over many years. Because of time constraints, the sweeping application of the wage-price freeze, and the paucity of procedural guides or standards in the Economic Stabilization Act, important elements of due process were undermined in the course of administering the program. During the freeze, prior publication of rules in the *Federal Register*, hearings and appeals procedure, and the other niceties of due process generally were ignored. This helped to create a strong sense of grievance among several groups—particularly organized labor—and made it difficult to enlist the continuing cooperation necessary for a long-term program. Some short-circuiting of due process is necessary and probably inevitable in the imposition of a wage-price freeze. With prior planning, however, at least rudimentary safeguards can and should be established to protect individual rights and to minimize the damage to existing institutional arrangements, such as collective bargaining and freedom of contract, that have been traditionally sanctioned by society.

Incomes Policy

Although the temptation to pass judgment is irresistible, the notion that a wage-price freeze has "succeeded" or "failed" within its own frame of reference misconstrues the basic function of a freeze as it relates to a general program of incomes policies. A technical assessment of the effectiveness of a wage-price freeze is of limited significance. Obviously, a freeze which enjoys wide public support and the full force of governmental authority can hold wages and prices steady over a short period unless the program flounders because of bureaucratic ineptness. However, the basic functions of a freeze relate less to the movement of wages and prices than to other considerations. The primary objectives of a freeze are to buy time to permit the development of more substantial economic policies and to influence expectations concerning the future course of wages and prices.

In a direct and abrupt manner, a wage-price freeze buys time to consider other alternatives. By definition, it seeks to proscribe wage and price increases for the designated period. As surprise action, it dramatically demonstrates the government's commitment to deal firmly, even ruthlessly, with inflation. To the extent that a freeze is hastily imposed in response to some immediate crisis, it may permit time to explore carefully other policies and to build the consensus necessary to sustain a long-term stabilization effort. In addition, a freeze may serve to dissipate political pressures and to restore some latitude to the national leadership. Certainly the wage-price freeze of 1971 fulfilled these objectives for the Nixon administration; it put an immediate brake on wages and prices while confounding critics and permitting the President to draw up the more detailed blueprints for Phase II in a supportive political environment.

The relationship of a wage-price freeze to expectations is more subtle and somewhat contradictory in nature. Although a freeze can suppress wage and price increases in the short run, even the most zealous advocate of incomes policies cannot expect that this situation will prevail indefinitely. Accordingly, a freeze will influence expectations not so much by its direct impact on wages and prices as by the assurance it provides that the government will adopt stern policies to cope with inflation in the post-freeze period. The expectations engendered by a freeze are more likely to relate to future governmental actions than to the immediate course of wage and price movements.

This linkage of expectations to future governmental actions may have a determinate effect on the shape of the post-freeze program. To the extent that a freeze has to be comprehensive and "tough" to be "successful," an expectation may be created that the post-freeze mechanism will be equally inclusive and resolute, so that the discretion of the economic policy makers is severely limited. And when the freeze is succeeded by another variant of incomes policy, the shape of the program may not be tailored to the economic circumstances. To be sure, the theory and practice of incomes policy may not be as advanced as that of acupuncture, but clearly a different mix of policies and mechanisms will be appropriate for different economic situations. A "tough," wide-ranging system of direct controls may be applicable to demand-pull inflation when the economy is operating at or near full capacity. Greater flexibility should be exercised in dealing with price inflation that reflects cost-push factors or shifts in power relationships in the economy. In both cases, some discrimination in coverage and standards will be necessary to deal with special economic circumstances. Hence one of the potential drawbacks of every wage-price freeze—especially when it is viewed as a "success"—is that it may lead to a post-freeze program somewhat inappropriate to the economic problems that it is designed to solve.

Such a series of events took place as an aftermath of the wage-price freeze of 1971. To allay a growing concern that the post-freeze program would be "soft" and beat a retreat from the advances made on August 15, the administration felt compelled to signal early in the freeze that Phase II would be comprehensive and would "have teeth." Initially Phase II lived up to this advance billing; the post-freeze stabilization program was indeed comprehensive and had complex mechanisms for enforcement. But was this desirable? Government economists had identified definite cost-push factors, not blanket causes, behind inflation. The coverage of Phase II should have been more discriminating and the means of enforcement more flexible. Considerable effort was subsequently expended by the Cost of Living Council to tailor the program more closely to the economic diagnosis through a cumulative process of exemption.[4]

A wage-price freeze is a sweeping, dramatic intervention by the government into the workings of the economy. Under some circumstances such an intervention can be the first step on a longer road to price stability. If implemented with discipline and skill, it can provide short-term benefits to the nation, as well as to economic policy makers and national political leaders. But intervention in the form of a wage-price freeze clearly is only the first step, and its most adroit use requires a judgment on what the ultimate destination will be and what course will be traveled to reach this goal.

---

4. The major cutback in coverage during Phase II was the exemption of all firms with 60 or less employees. In addition the Cost of Living Council exempted the wages and salaries of professional athletes and federal employees. Under a provision of the Economic Stabilization Act all members of the "working poor," or those earning less than $2.75 per hour, were also exempted.

Index

133